TWO MOVES CHESS

BOOK GAMES FOR KIDS AND BEGINNERS

Puzzle 1

White to move

Knight f6
Queen h7
Black
King h8

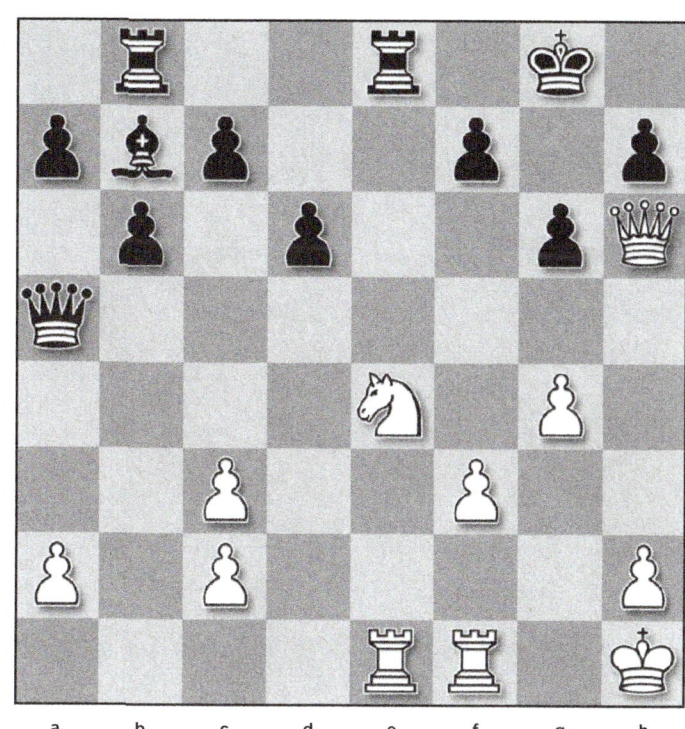

Puzzle 2

White to move

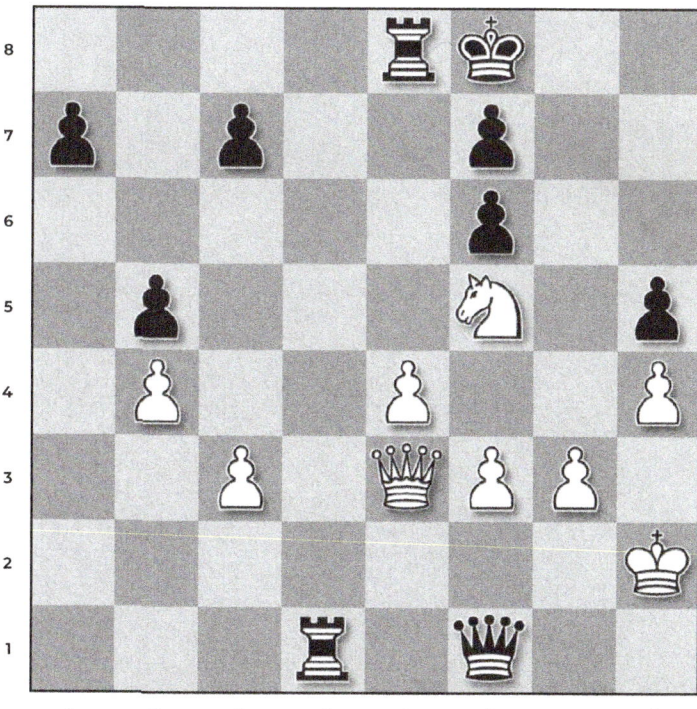

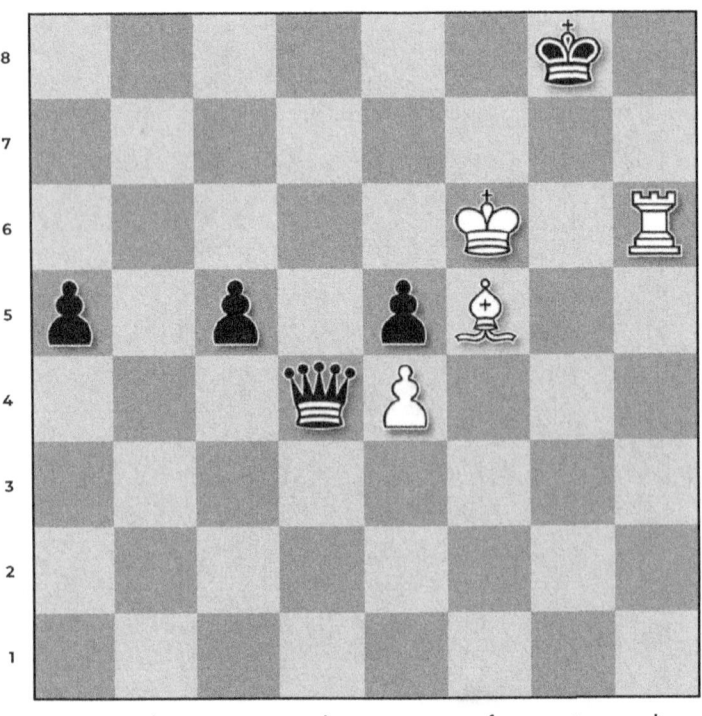

Puzzle 3
White to move

Puzzle 4
White to move

Puzzle 5

White to move

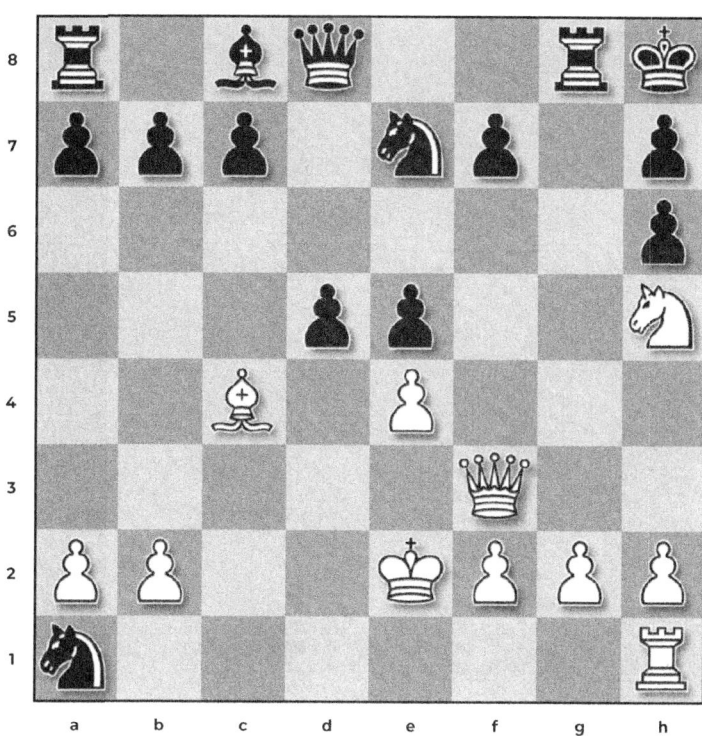

Puzzle 6

White to move

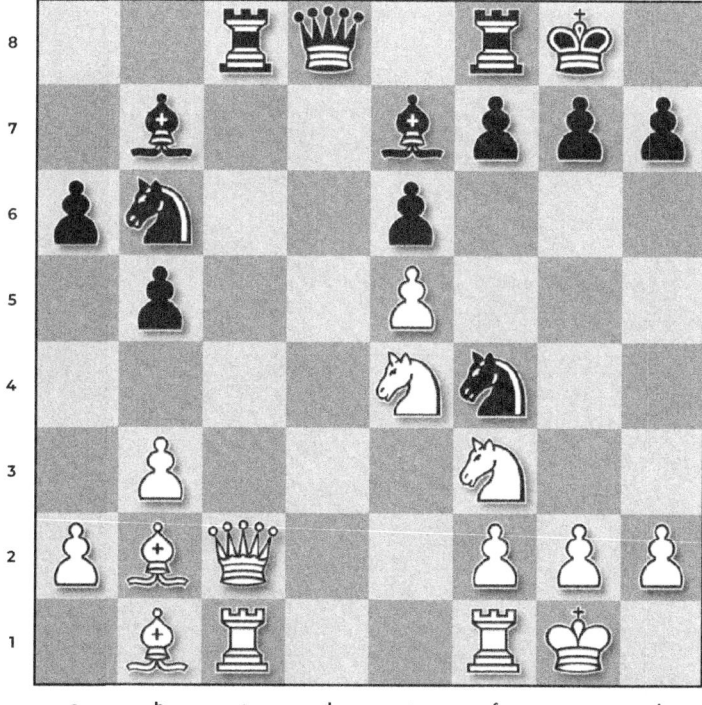

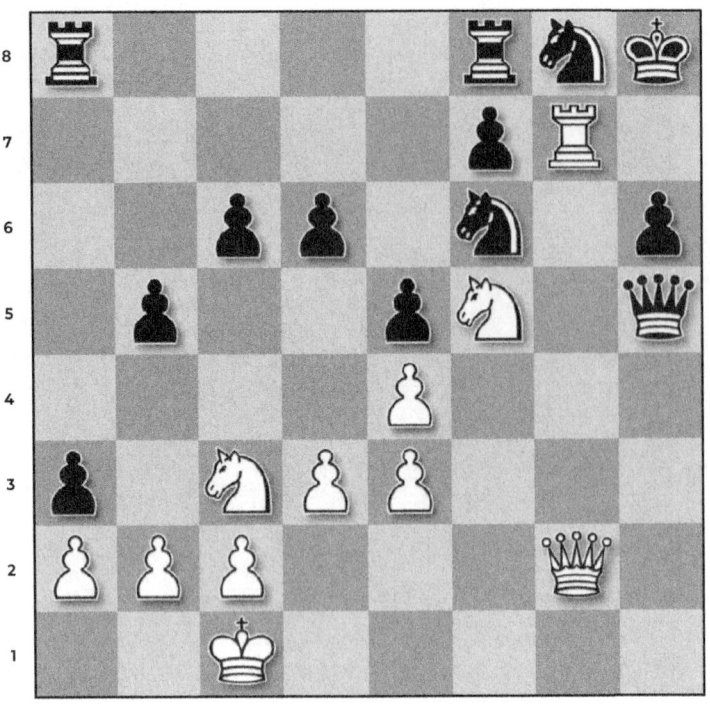

Puzzle 7
White to move

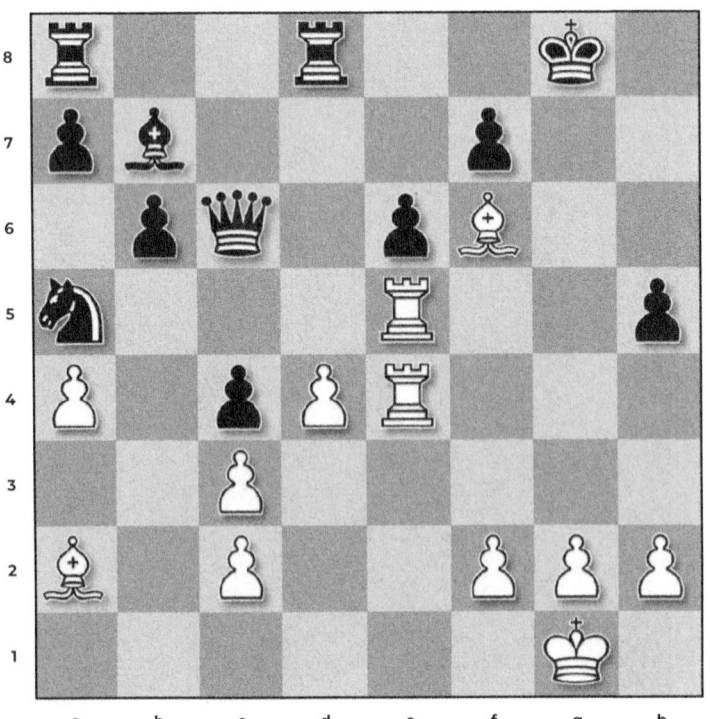

Puzzle 8
White to move

Puzzle 9
White to move

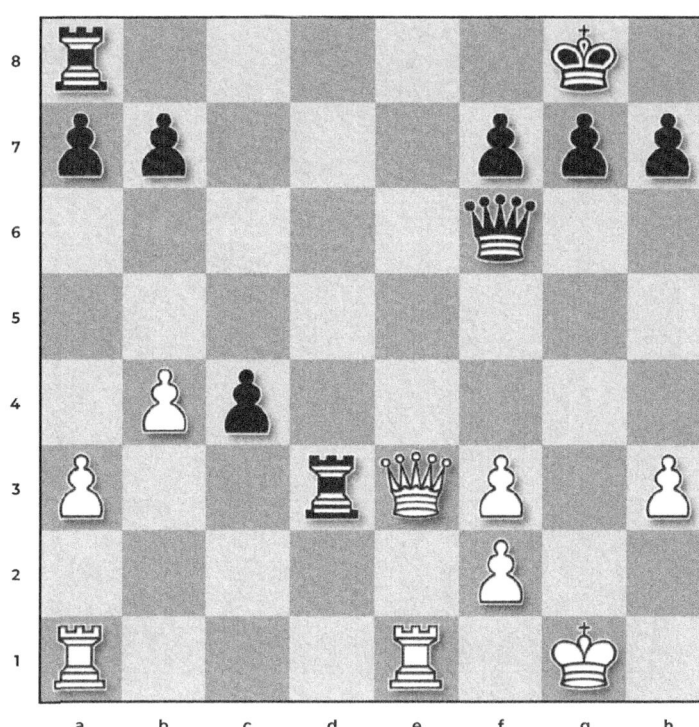

Puzzle 10
White to move

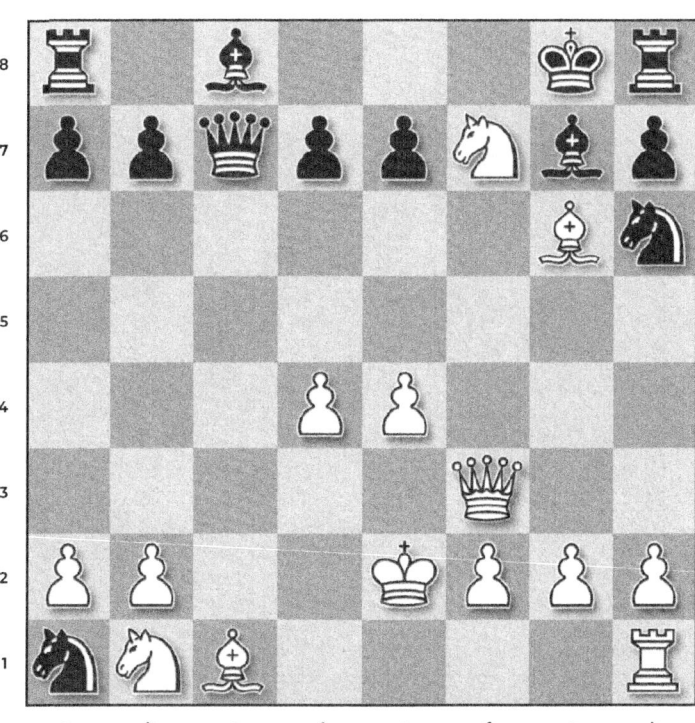

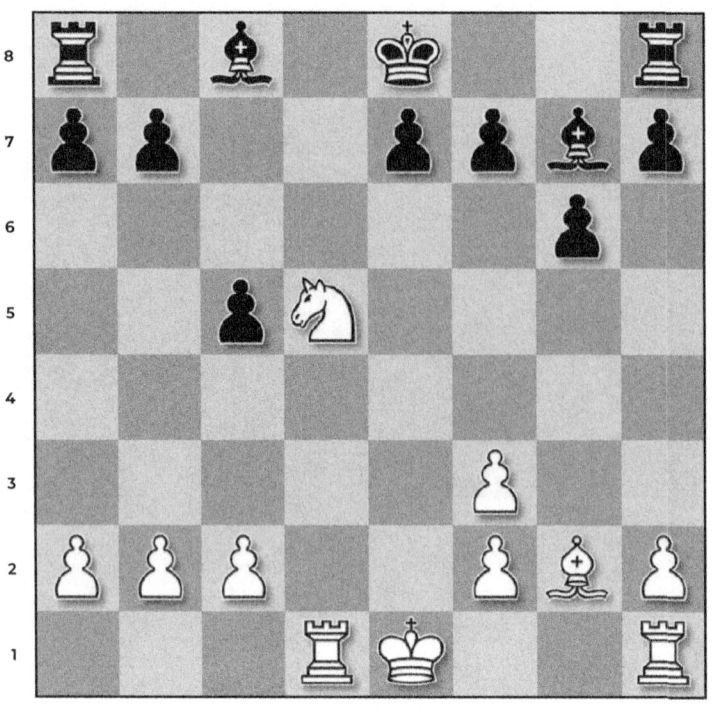

Puzzle 11
White to move

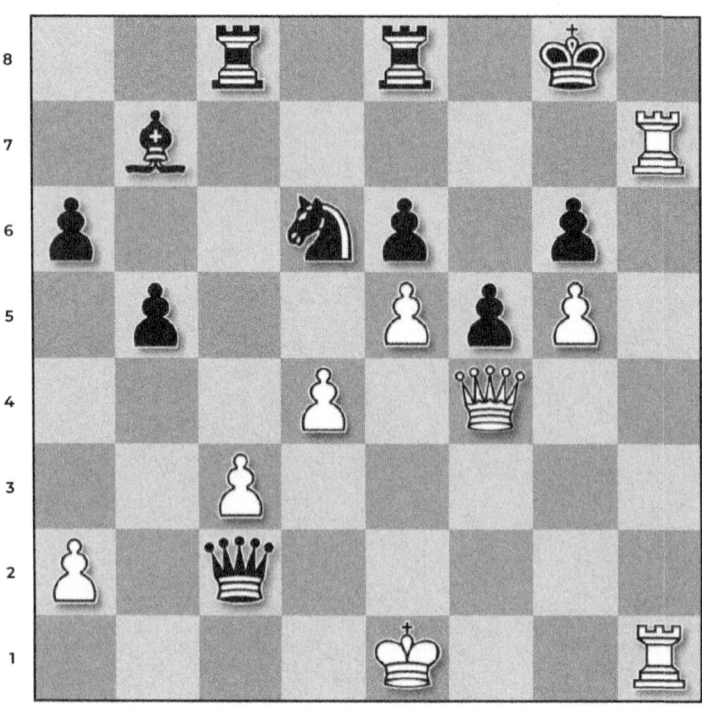

Puzzle 12
White to move

Puzzle 13

White to move

Puzzle 14

White to move

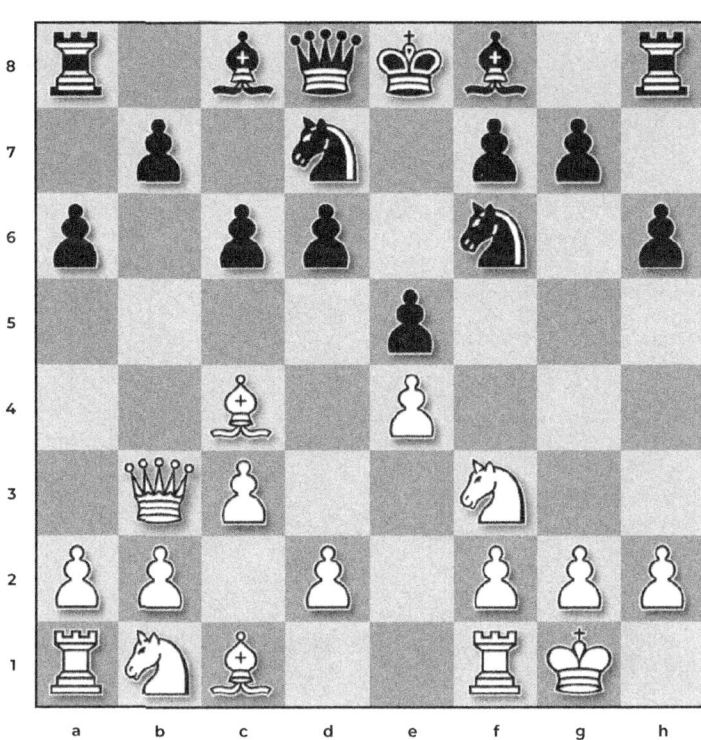

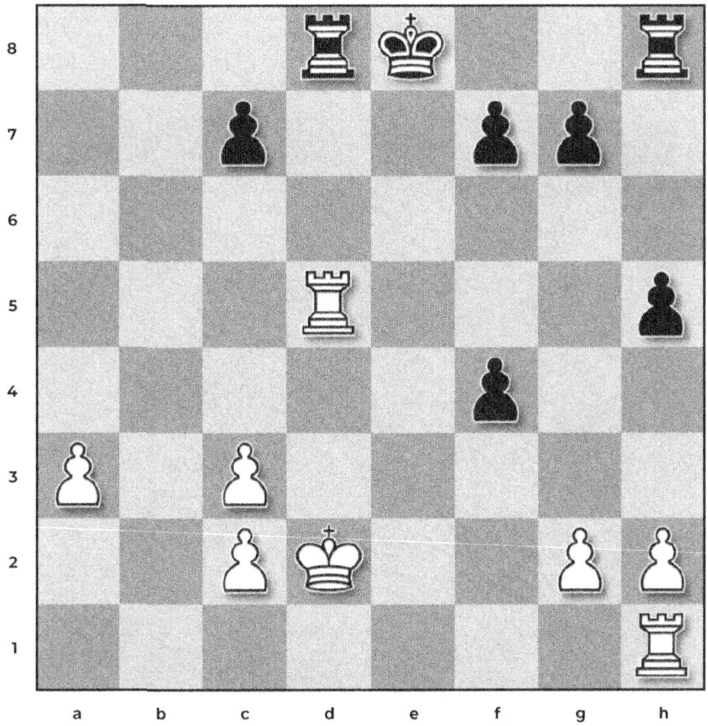

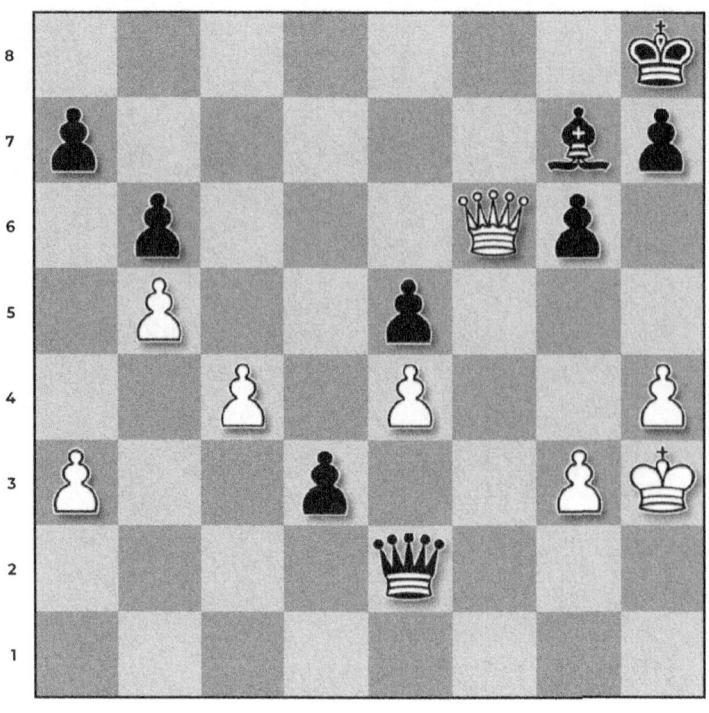

Puzzle 15
White to move

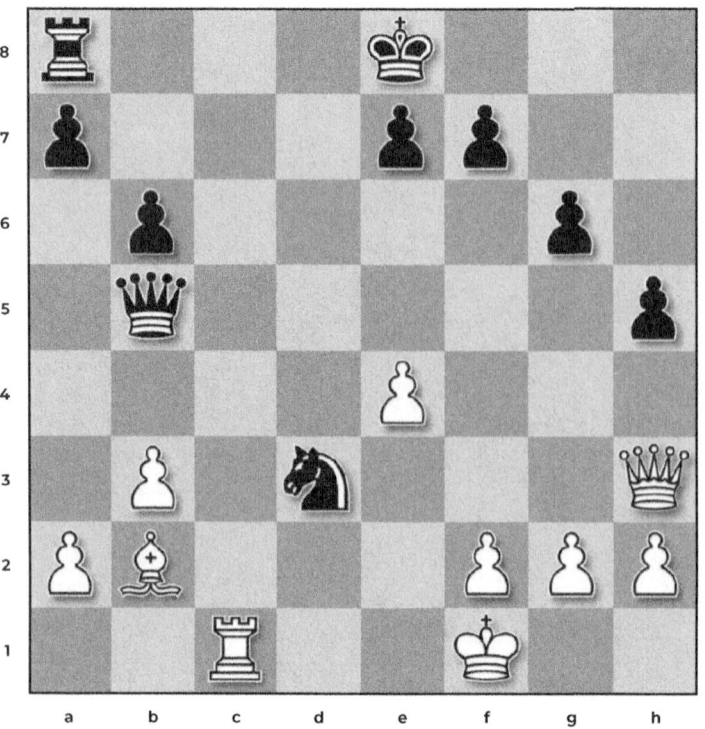

Puzzle 16
White to move

Puzzle 17

White to move

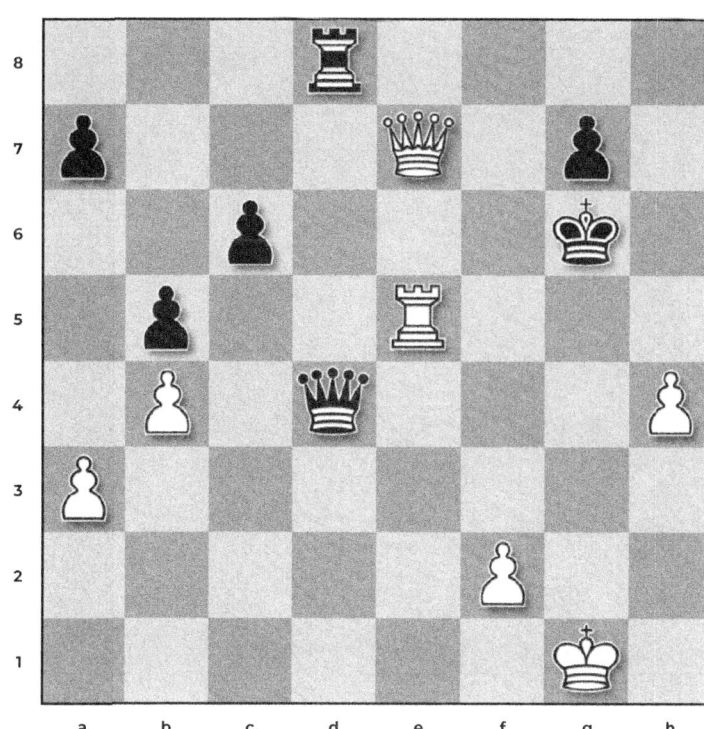

Puzzle 18

White to move

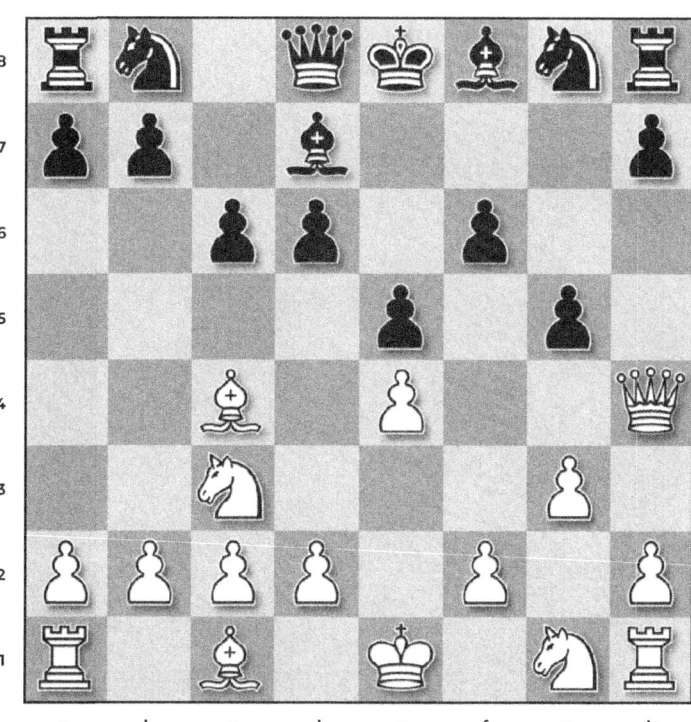

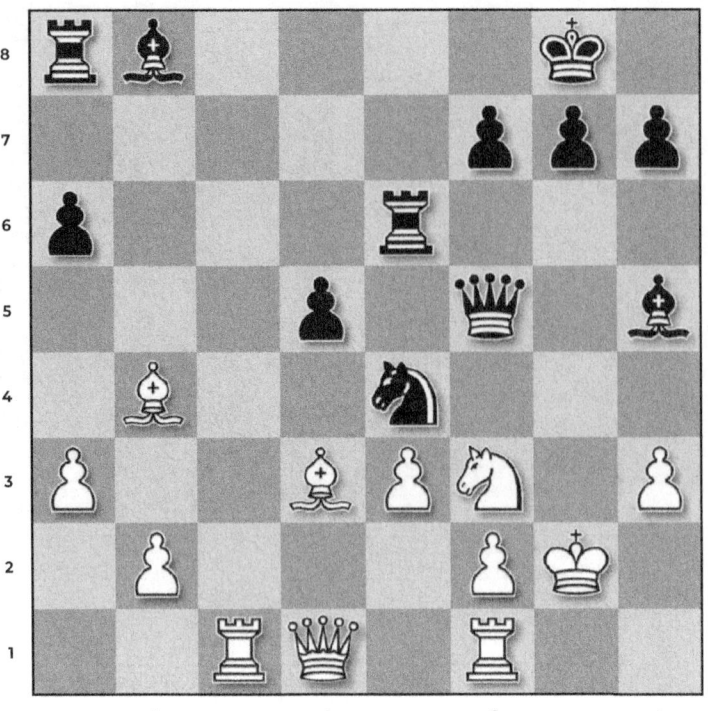

Puzzle 19
White to move

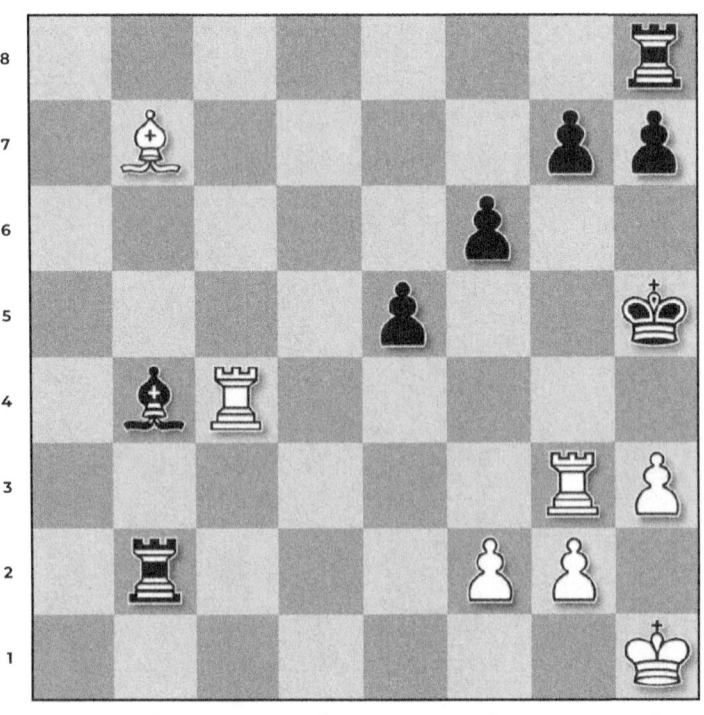

Puzzle 20
White to move

Puzzle 21
White to move

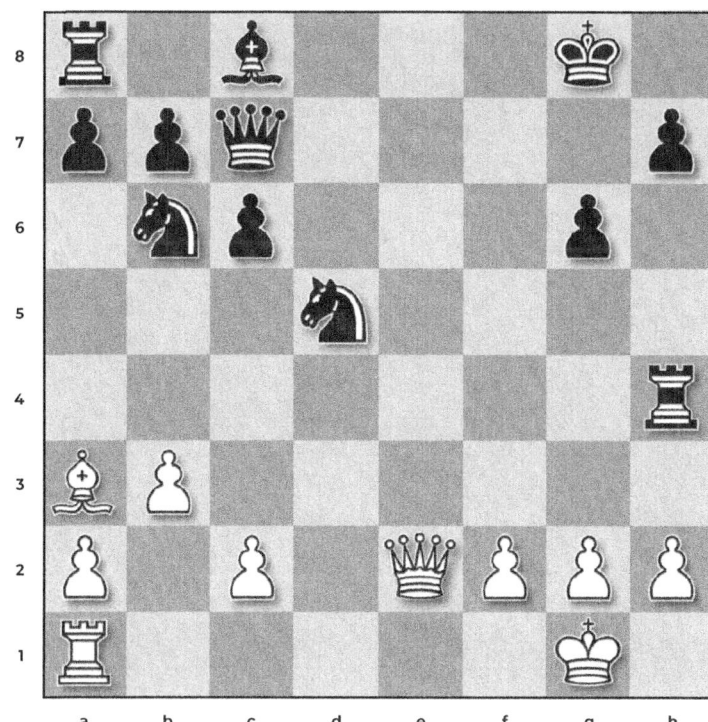

Puzzle 22
White to move

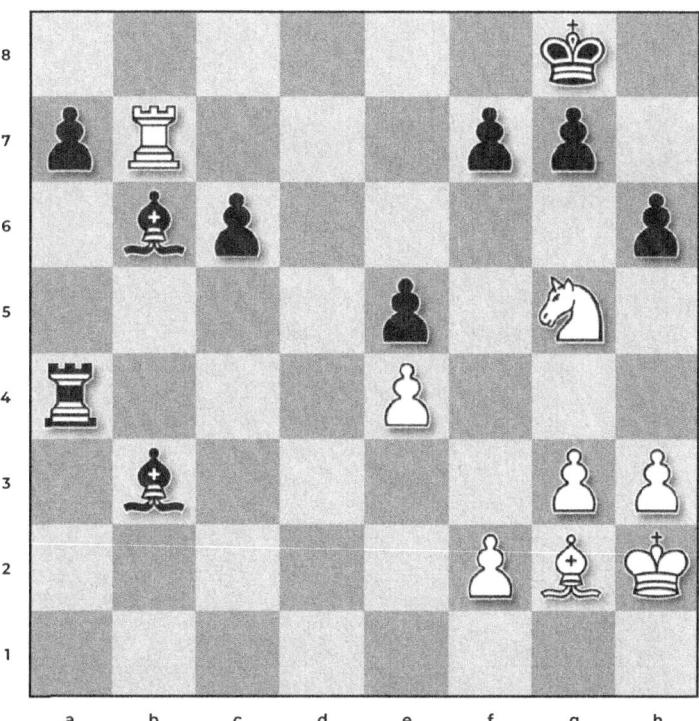

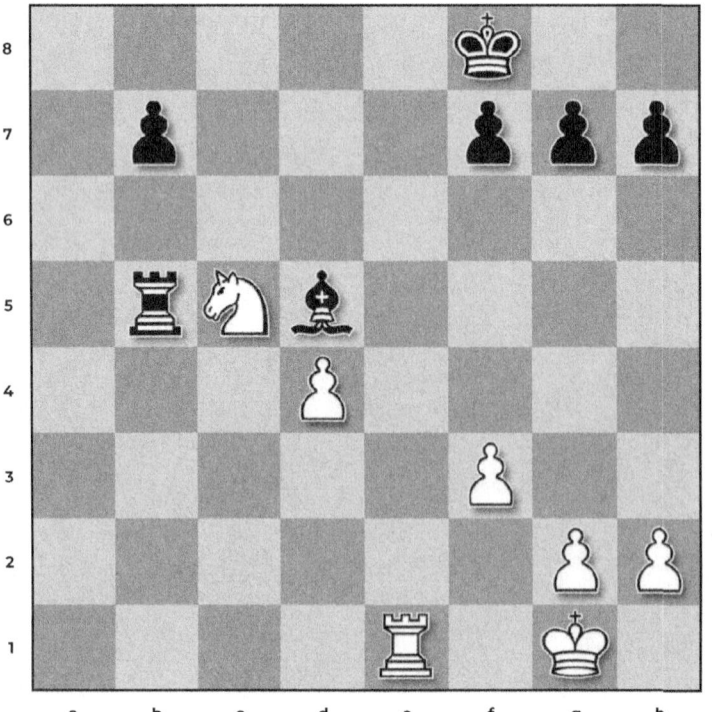

Puzzle 23
White to move

Puzzle 24
White to move

Puzzle 25
White to move

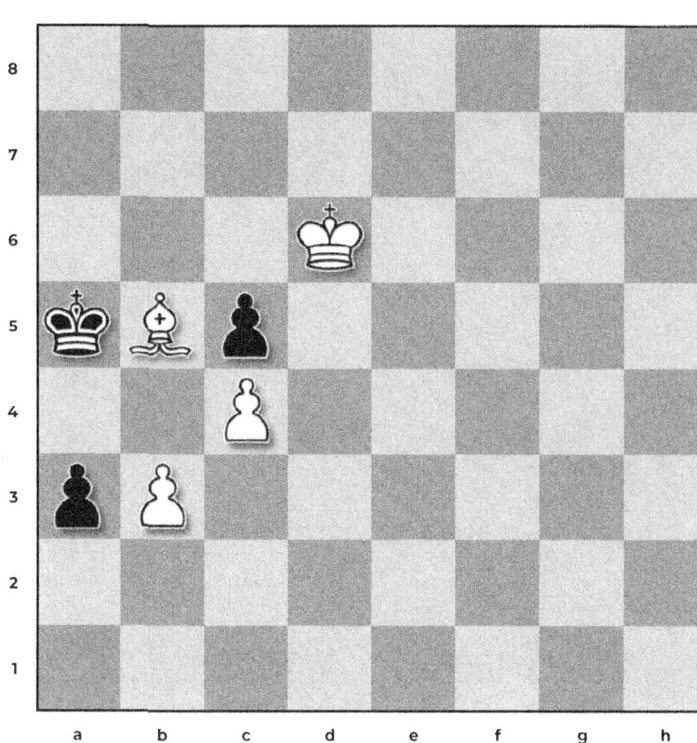

Puzzle 26
White to move

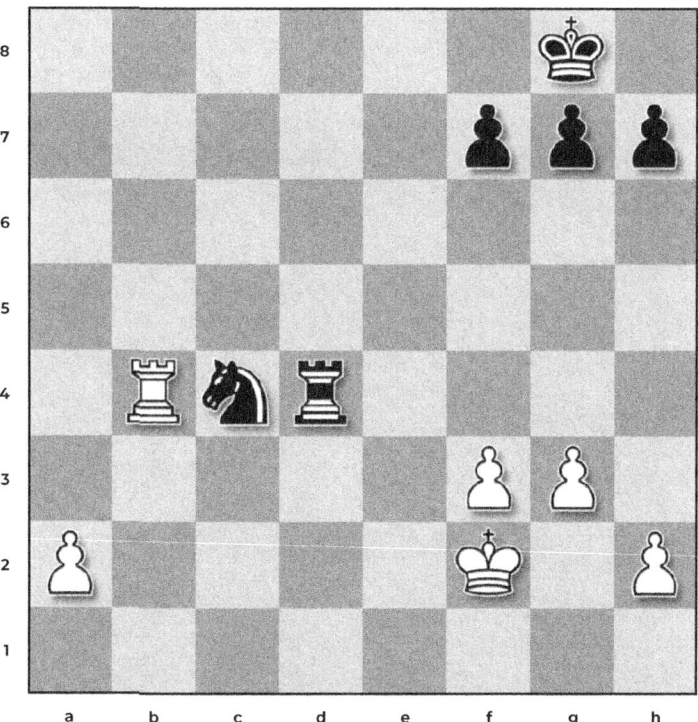

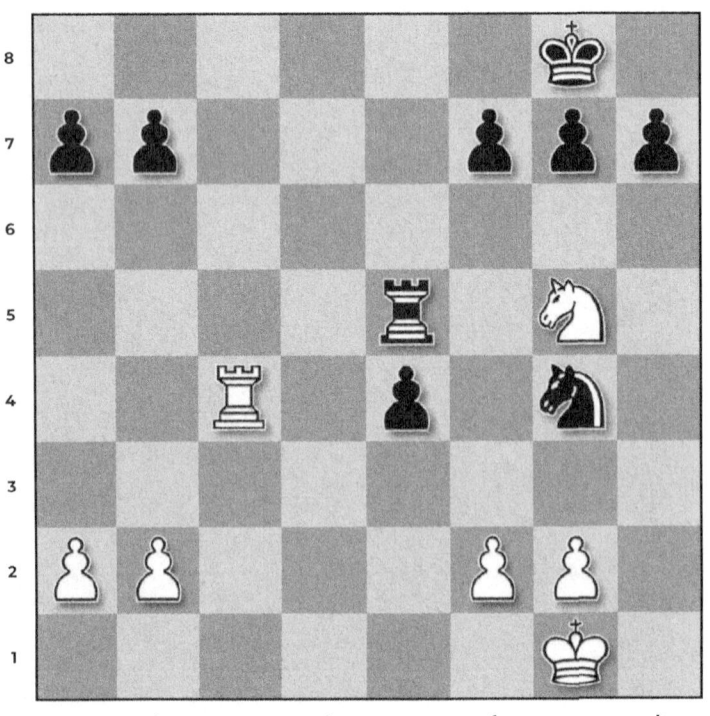

Puzzle 27

White to move

Puzzle 28

White to move

Puzzle 29
White to move

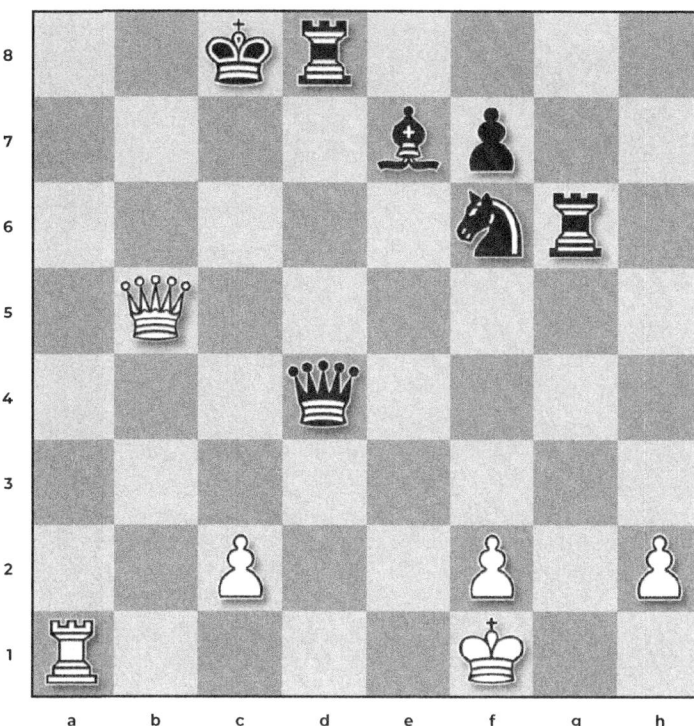

Puzzle 30
White to move

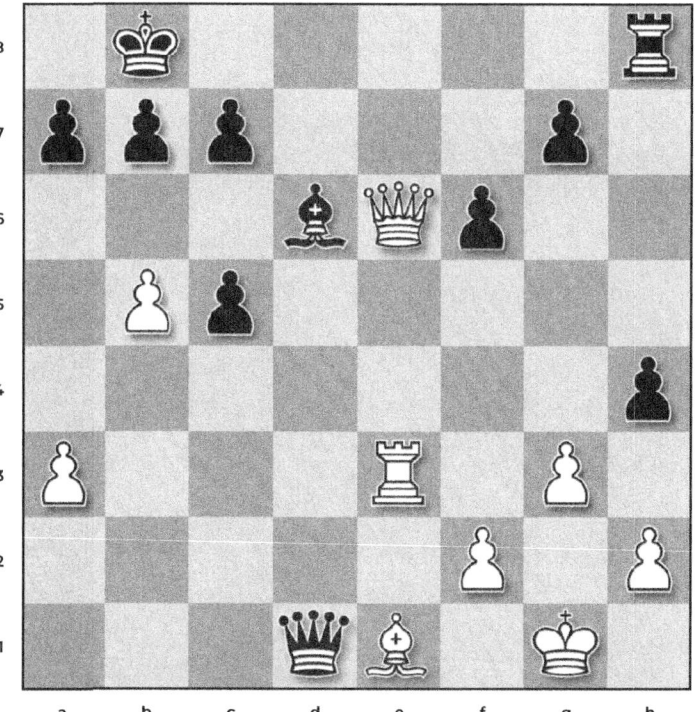

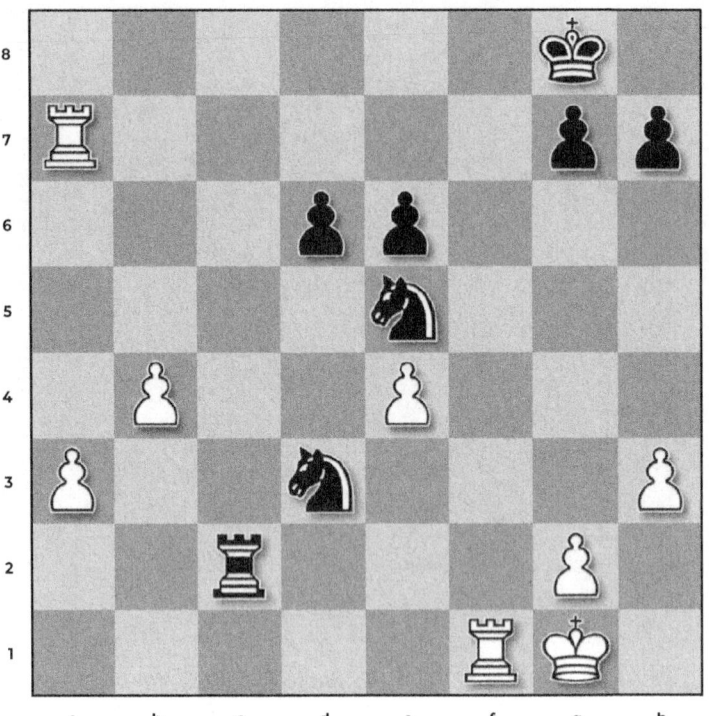

Puzzle 31

White to move

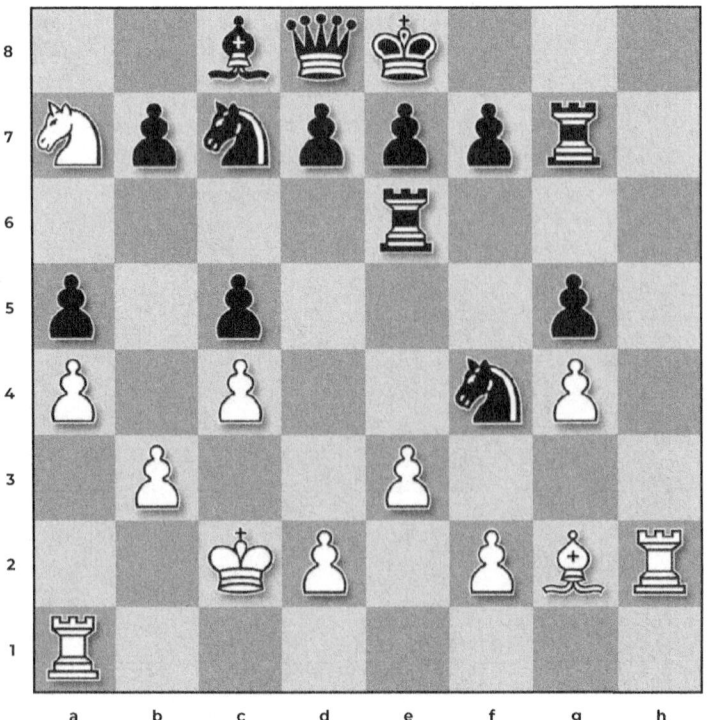

Puzzle 32

White to move

Puzzle 33
White to move

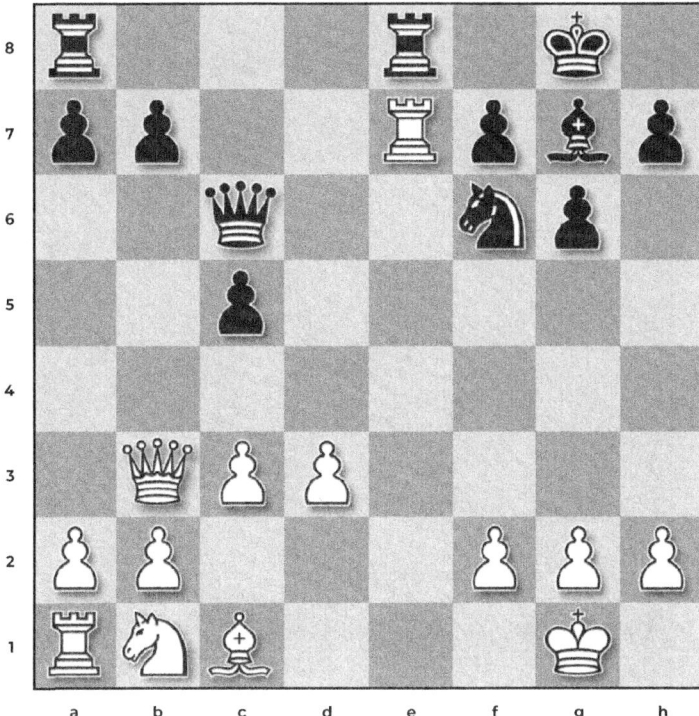

Puzzle 34
White to move

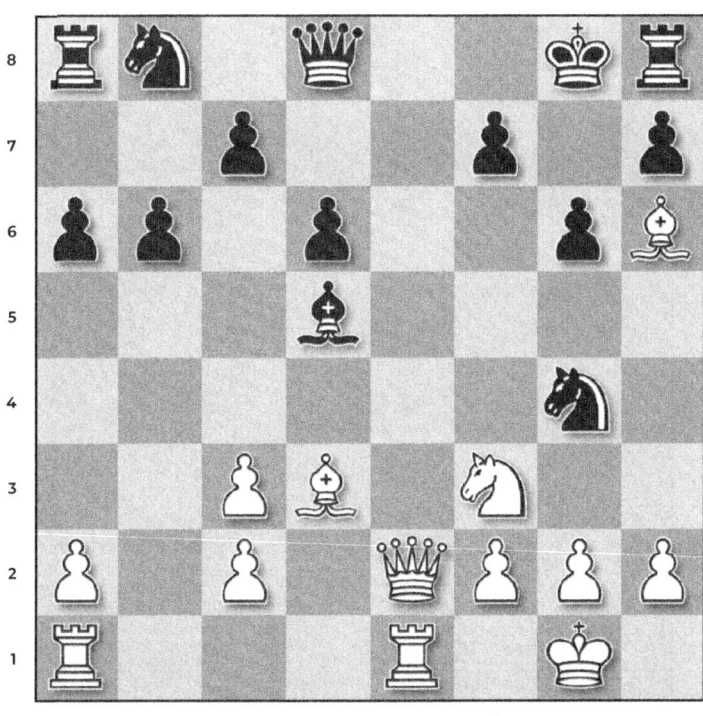

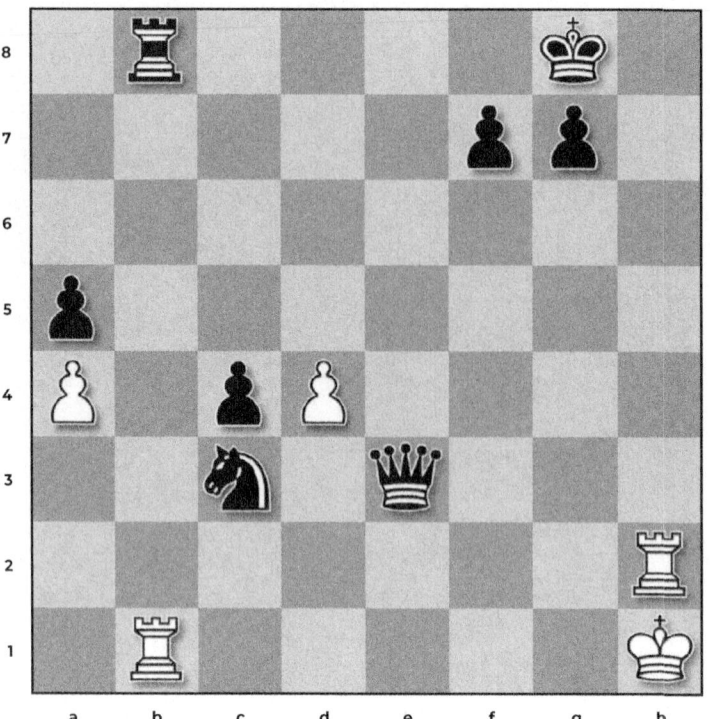

Puzzle 35
White to move

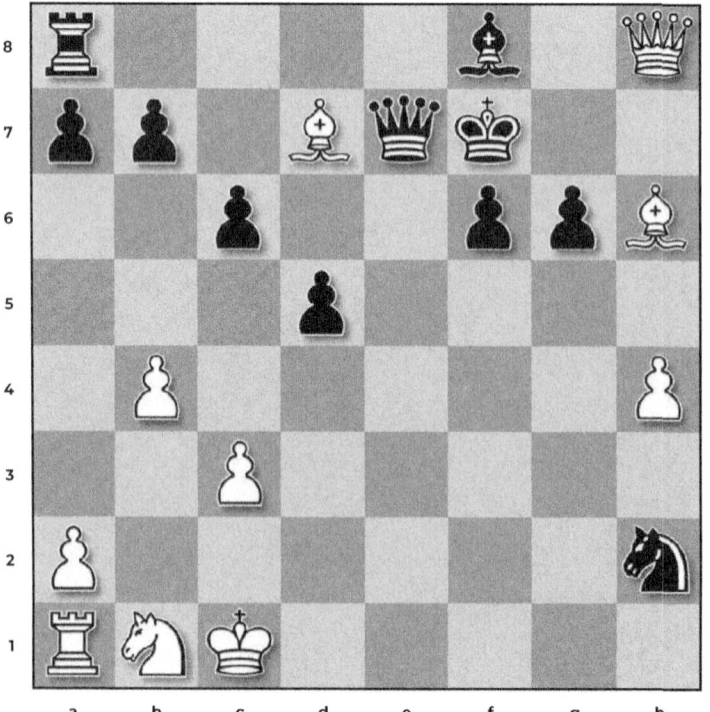

Puzzle 36
White to move

Puzzle 37
White to move

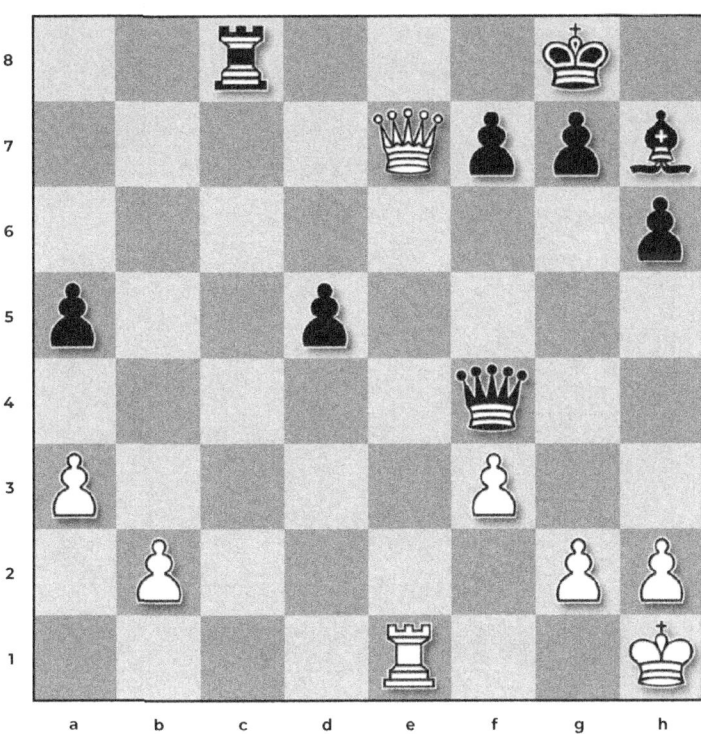

Puzzle 38
White to move

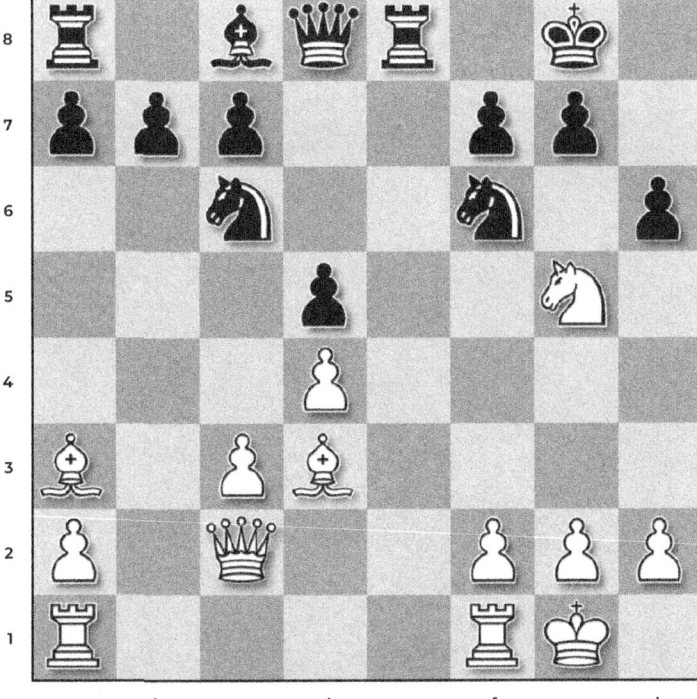

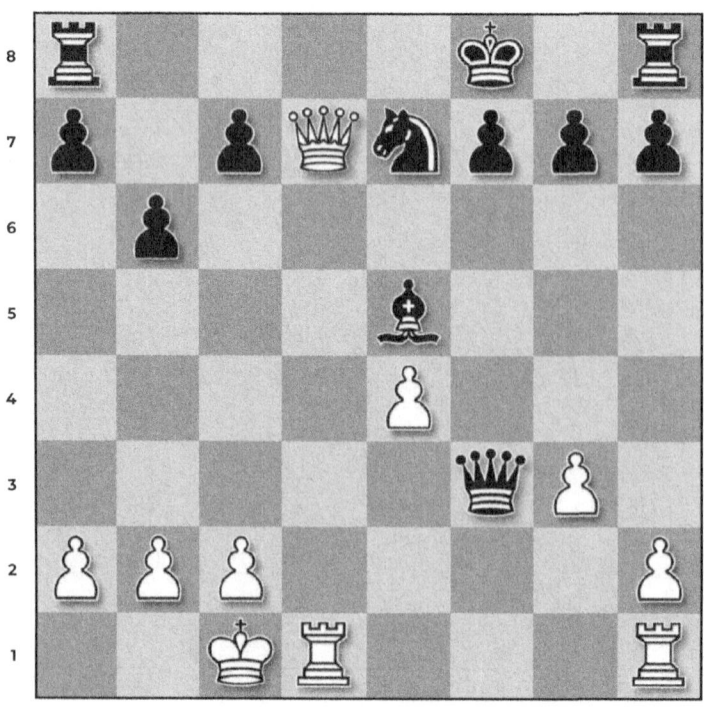

Puzzle 39
White to move

Puzzle 40
White to move

Puzzle 41
White to move

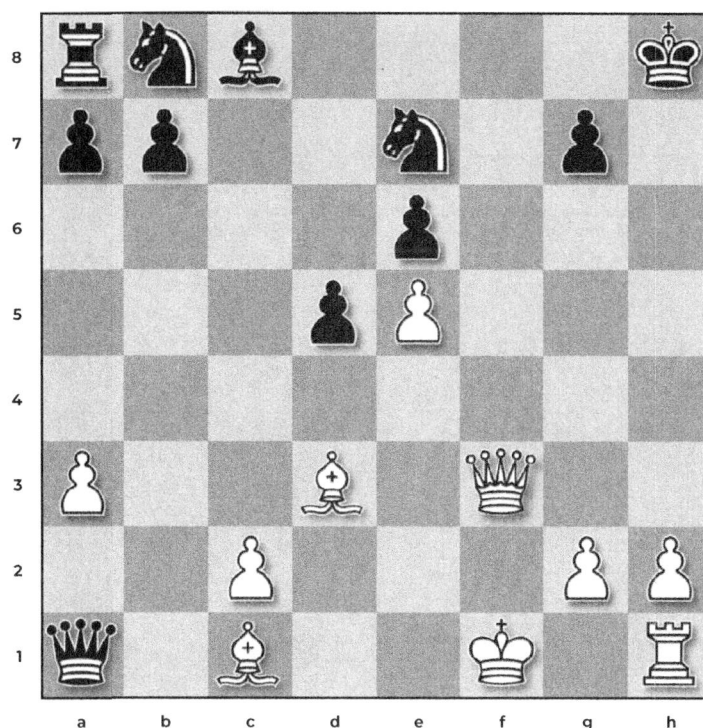

Puzzle 42
White to move

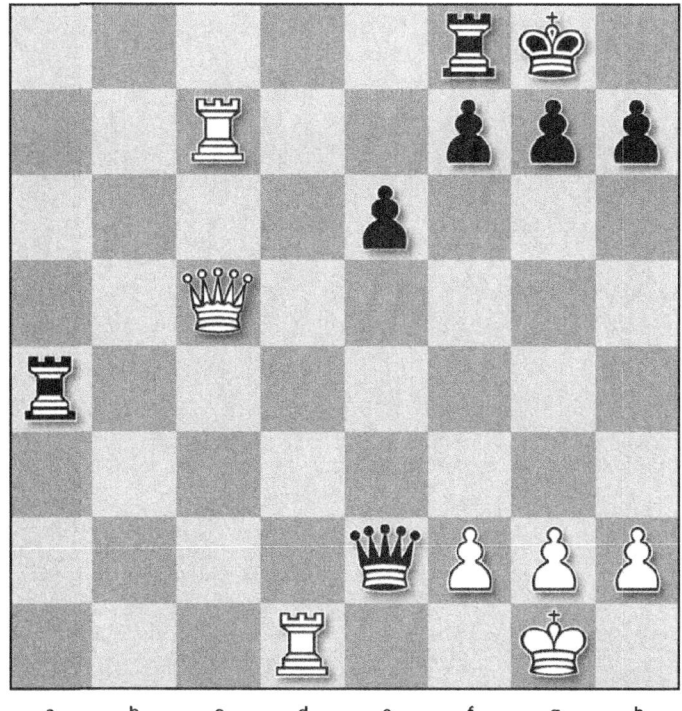

Puzzle 43
White to move

Puzzle 44
White to move

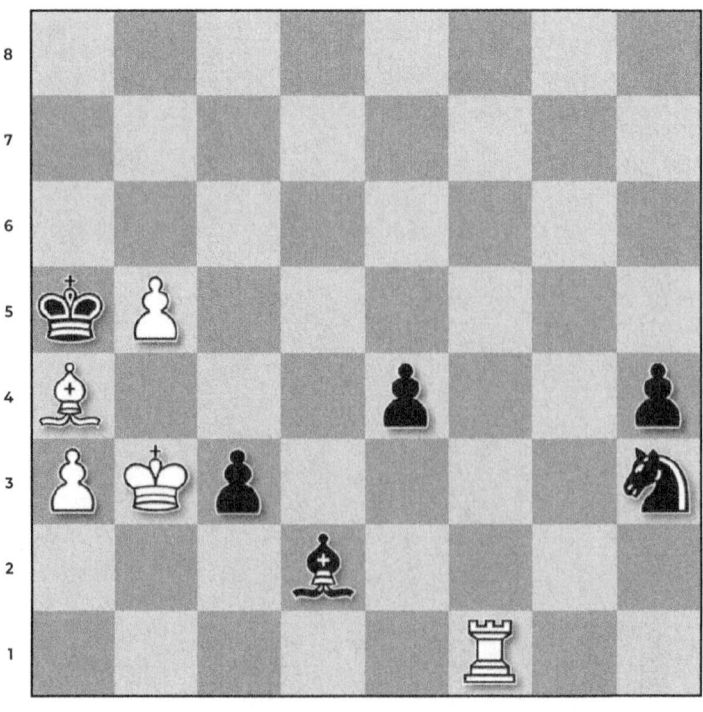

Puzzle 45

White to move

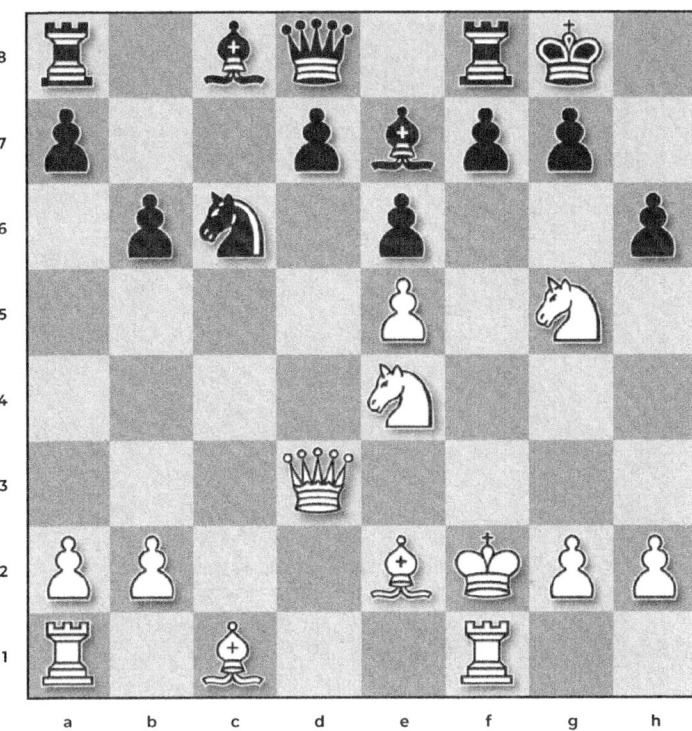

Puzzle 46

White to move

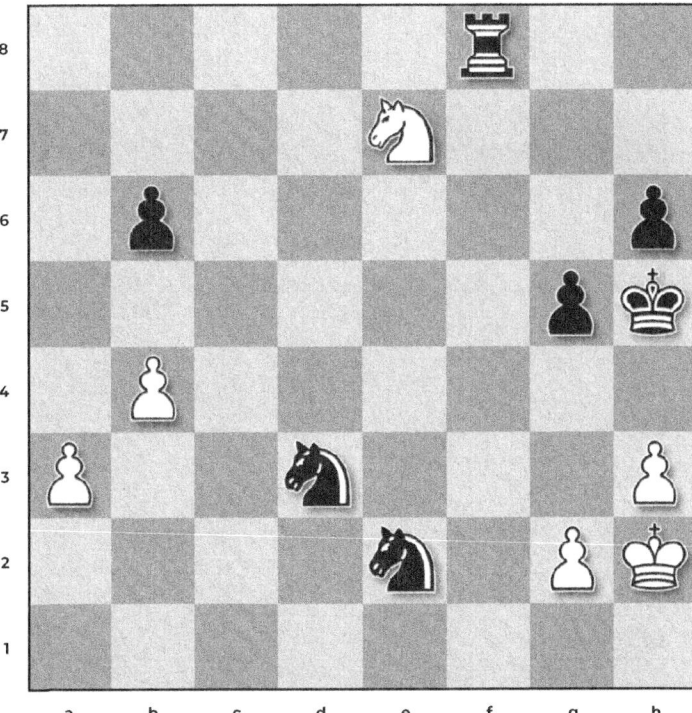

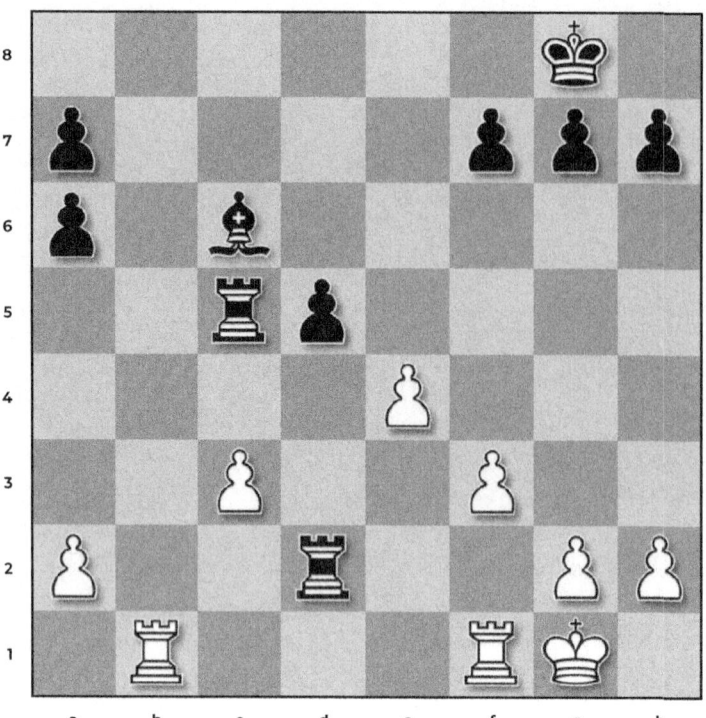

Puzzle 47
White to move

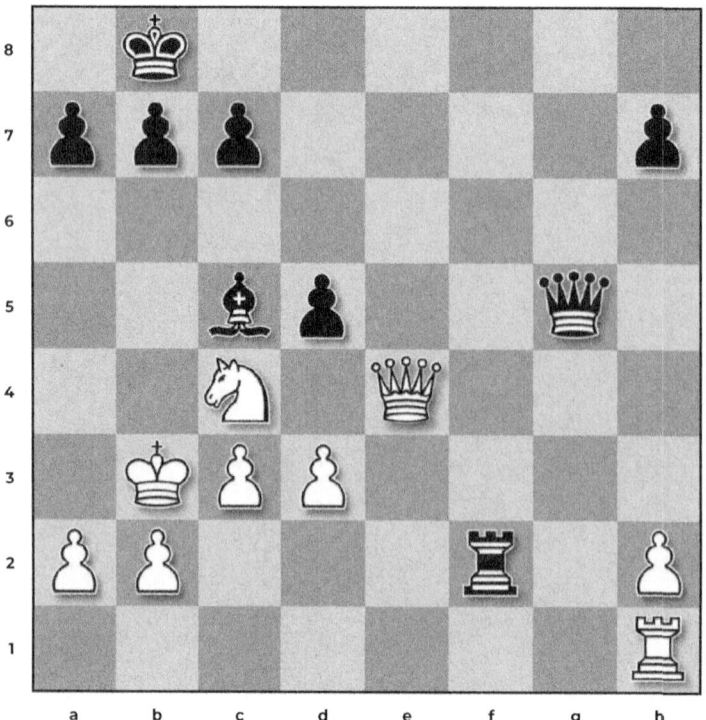

Puzzle 48
White to move

Puzzle 49
White to move

Puzzle 50
White to move

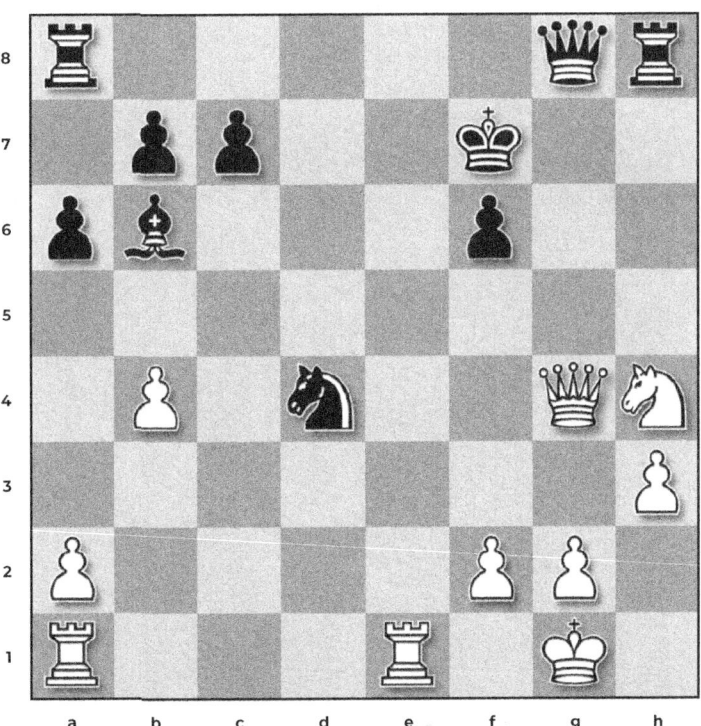

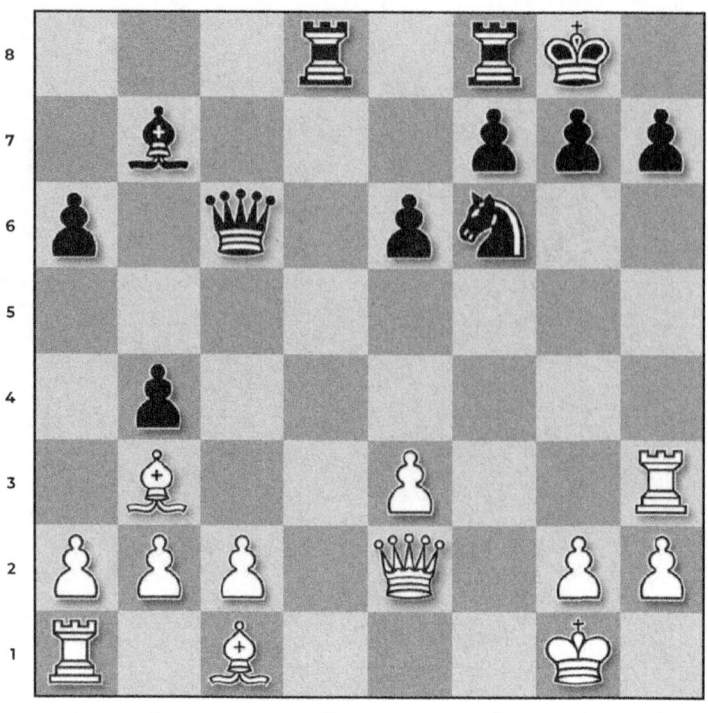

Puzzle 51

Black to move

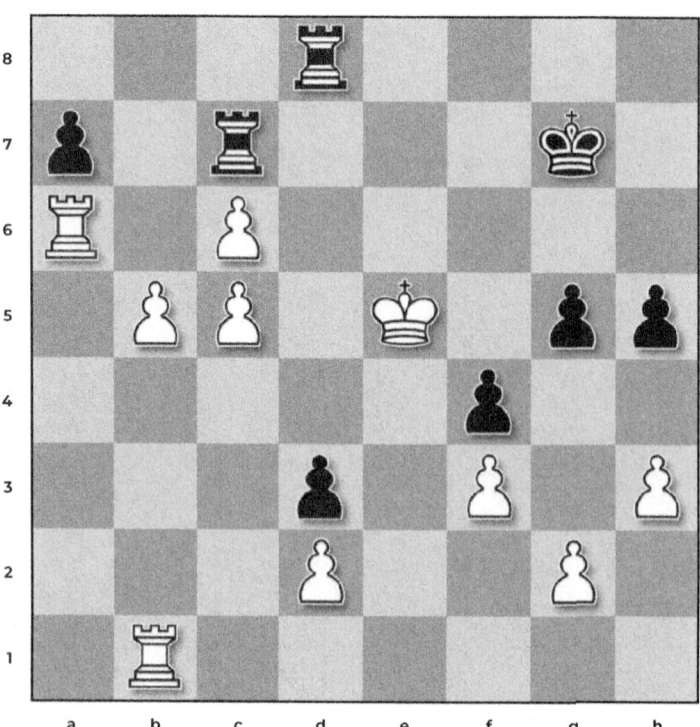

Puzzle 52

Black to move

Puzzle 53

Black to move

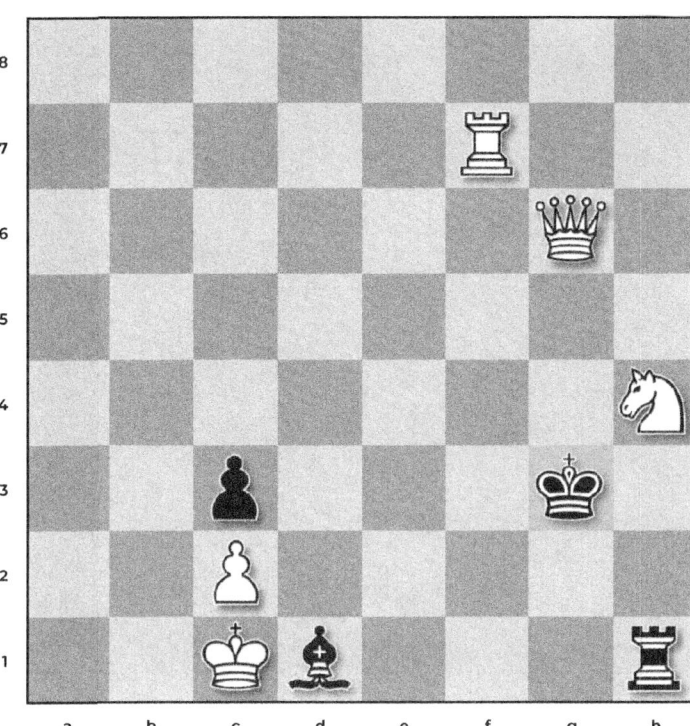

Puzzle 54

Black to move

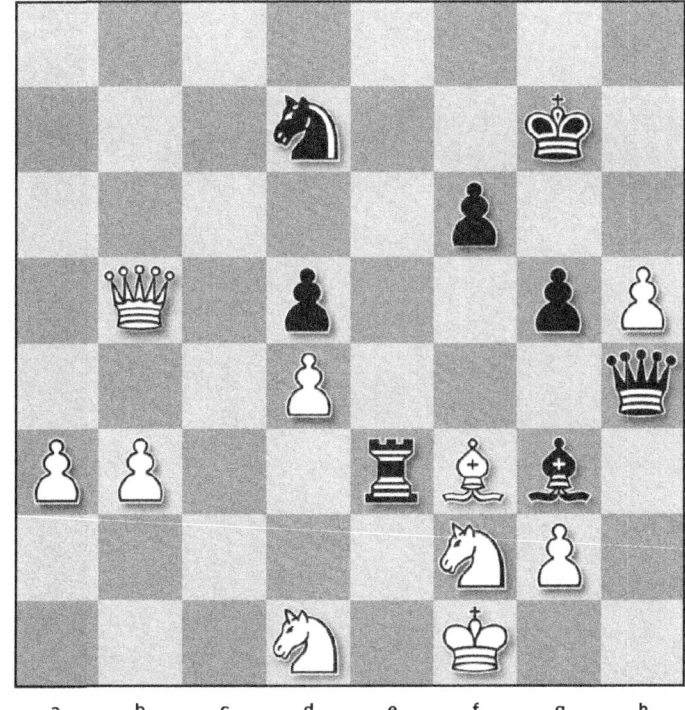

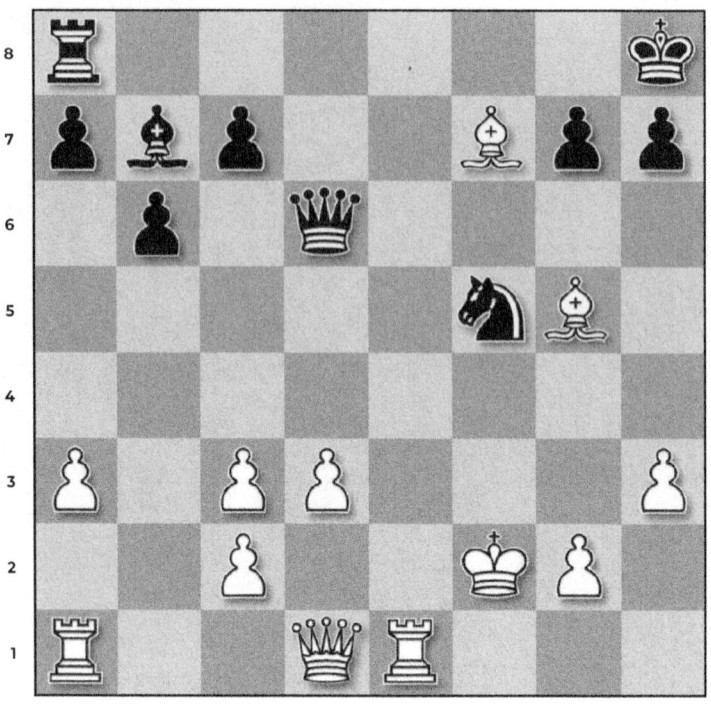

Puzzle 55
Black to move

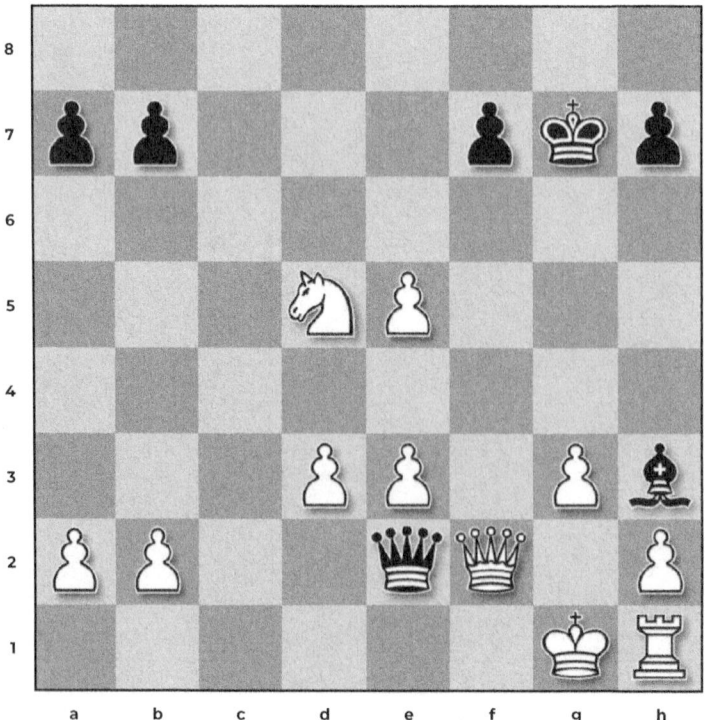

Puzzle 56
Black to move

Puzzle 57

Black to move

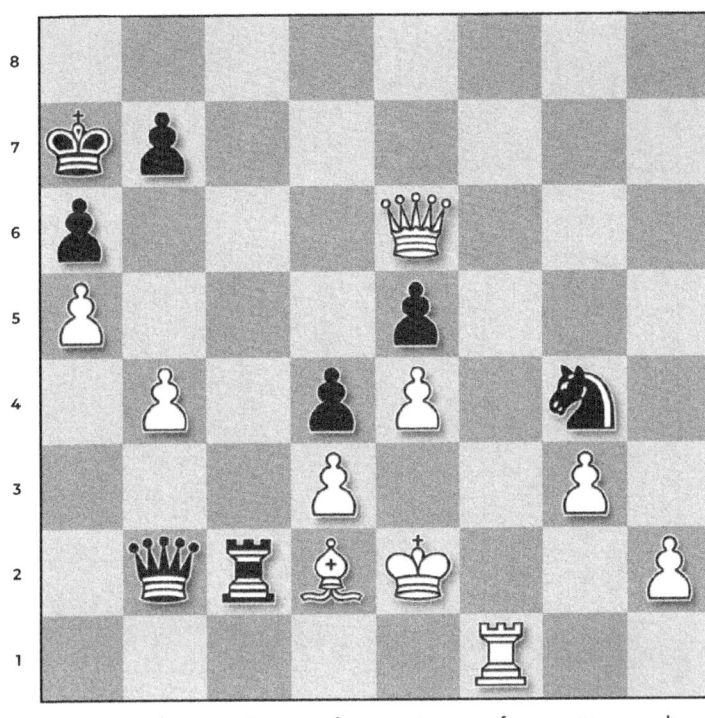

Puzzle 58

Black to move

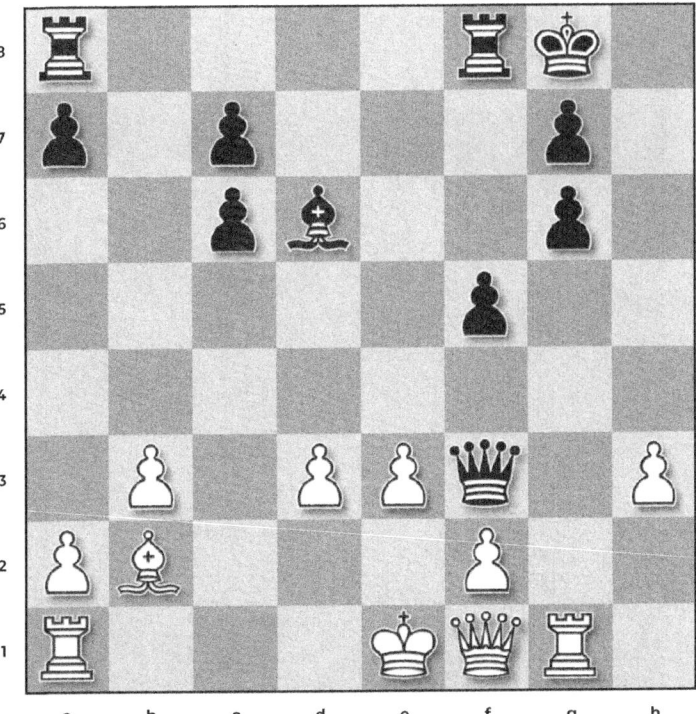

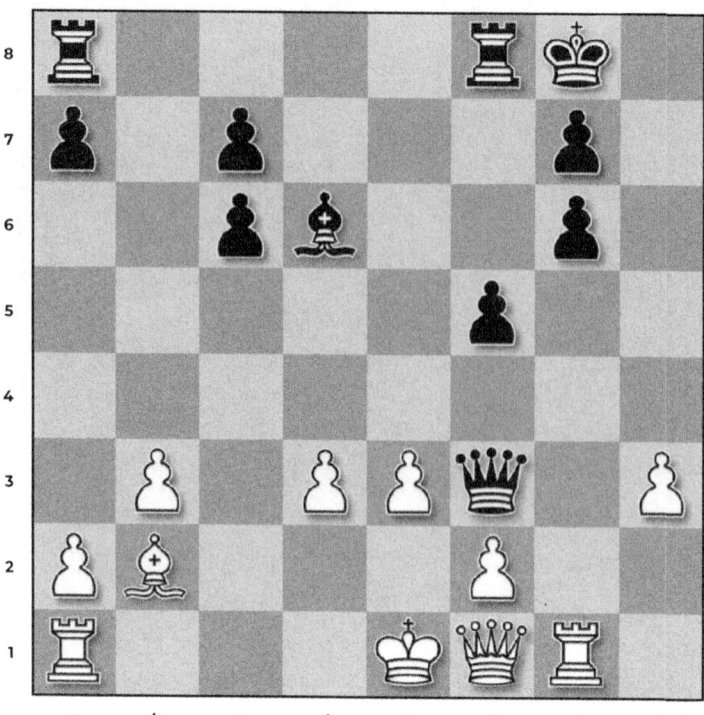

Puzzle 59

Black to move

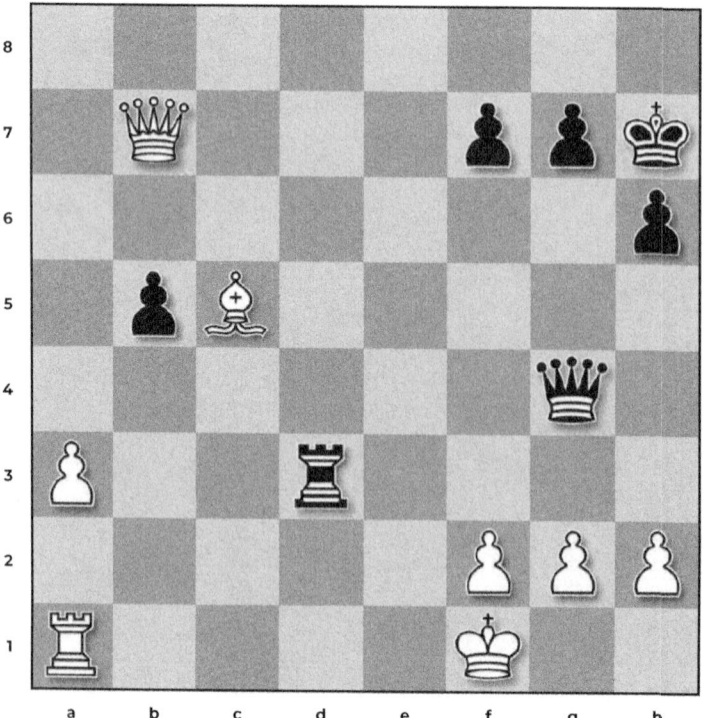

Puzzle 60

Black to move

Puzzle 61

Black to move

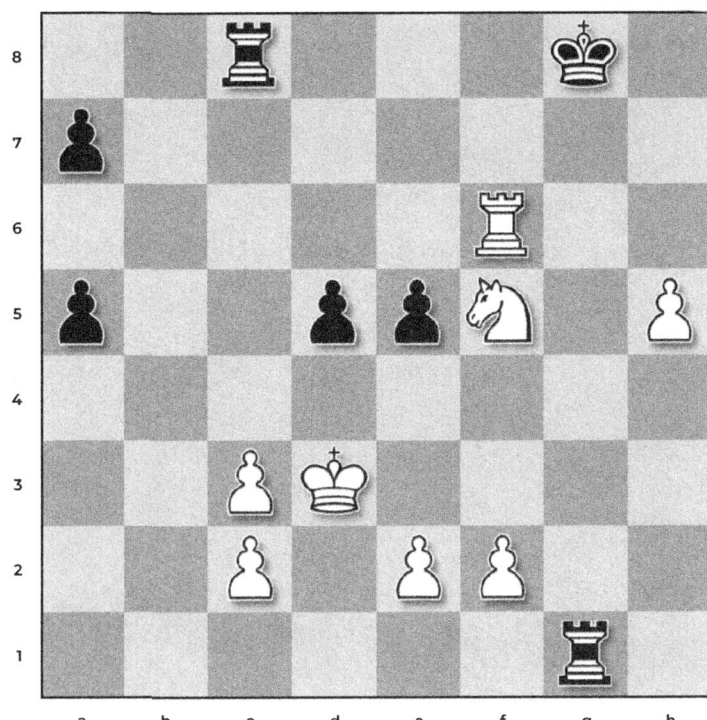

Puzzle 62

Black to move

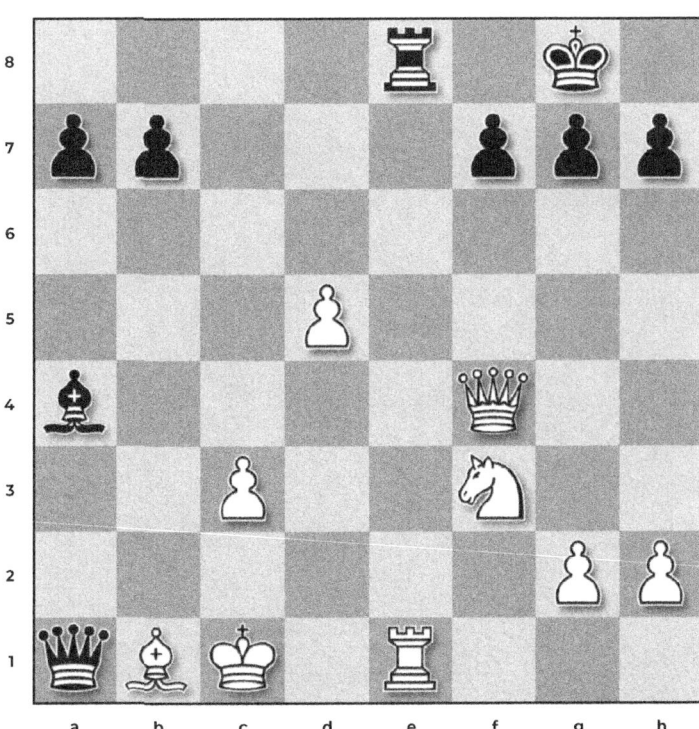

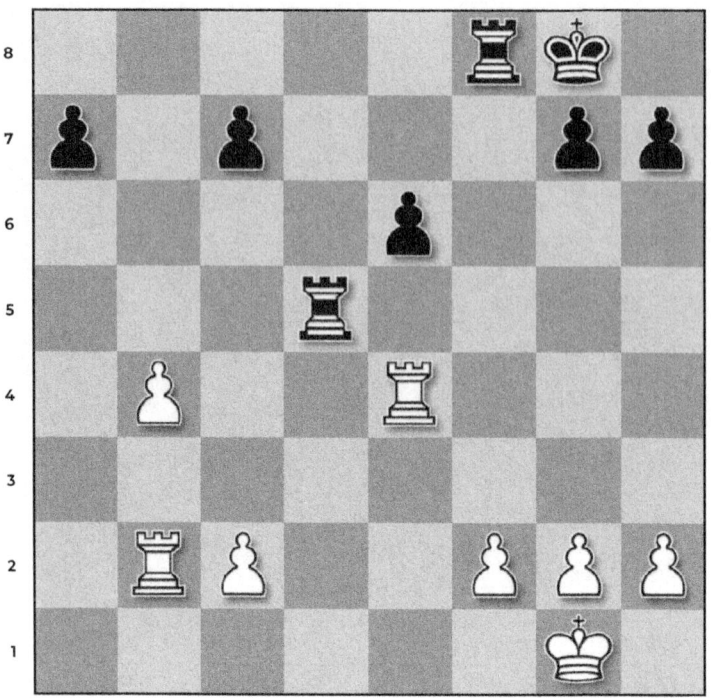

Puzzle 63

Black to move

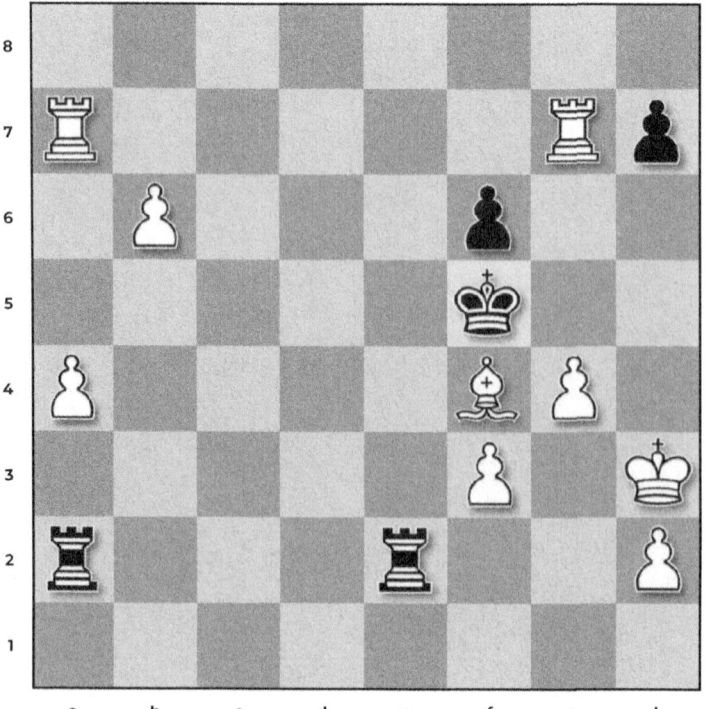

Puzzle 64

Black to move

Puzzle 65

Black to move

Puzzle 66

Black to move

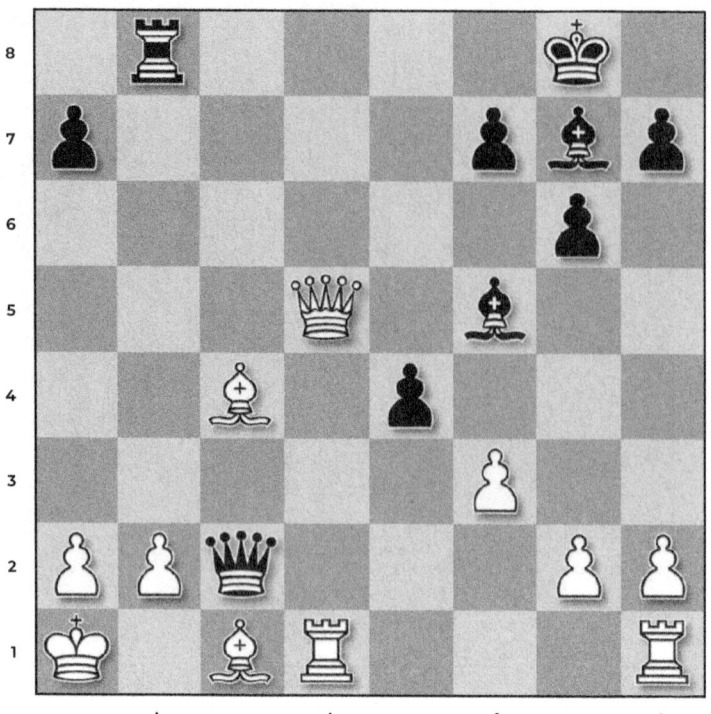

Puzzle 67
Black to move

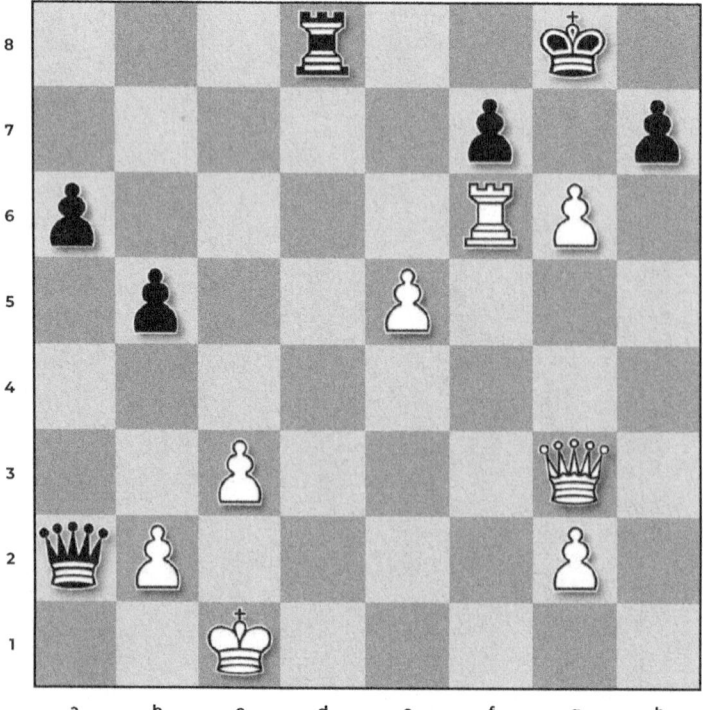

Puzzle 68
Black to move

Puzzle 69

Black to move

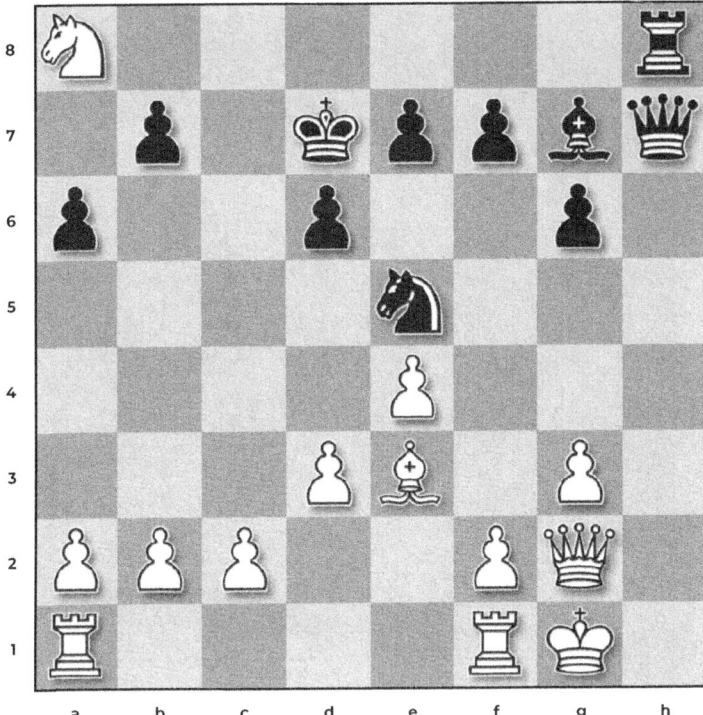

Puzzle 70

Black to move

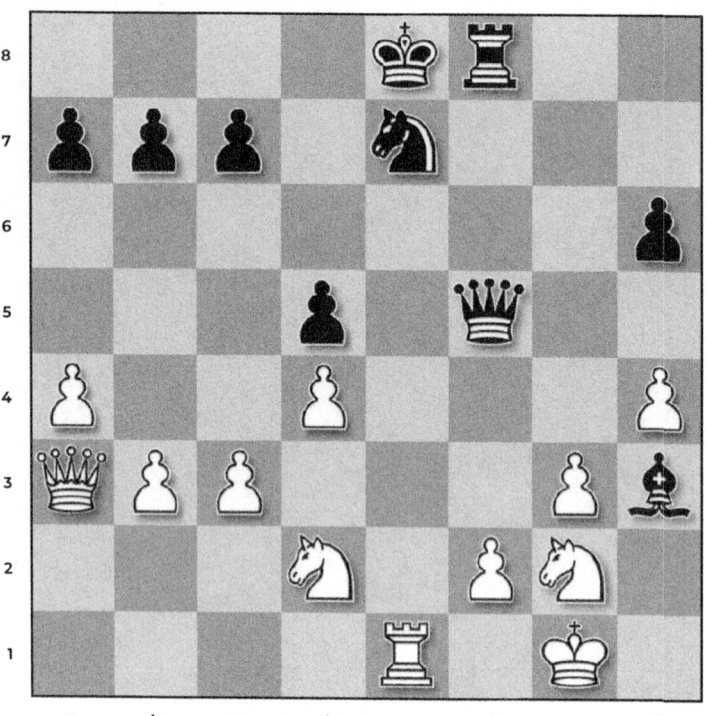

Puzzle 71

Black to move

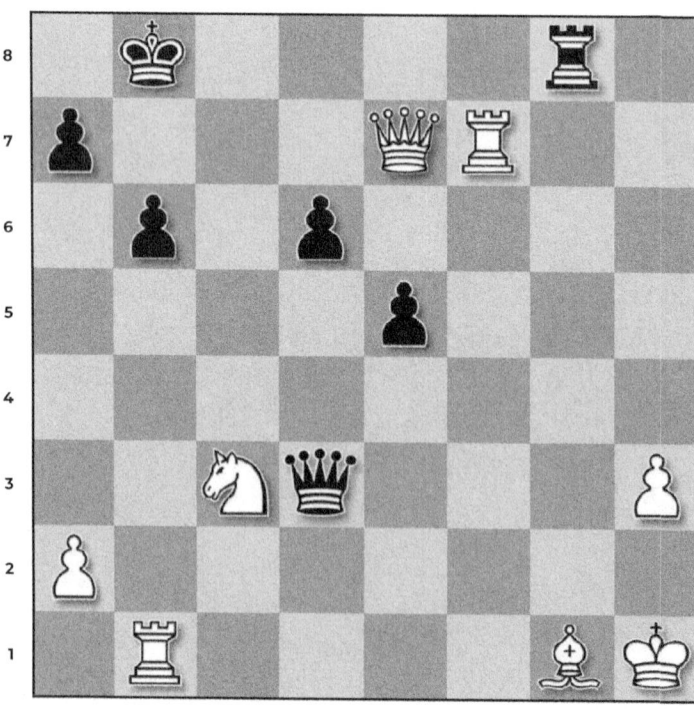

Puzzle 72

Black to move

Puzzle 73

Black to move

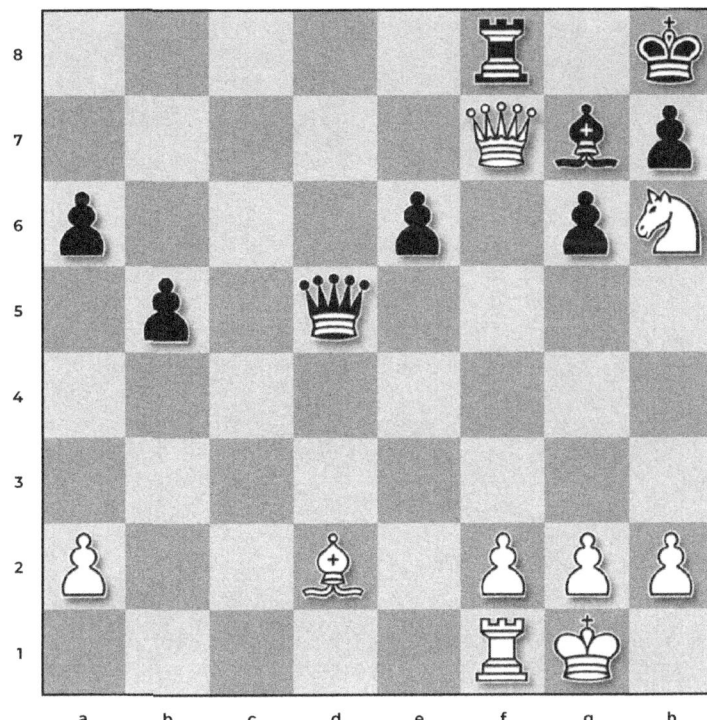

Puzzle 74

Black to move

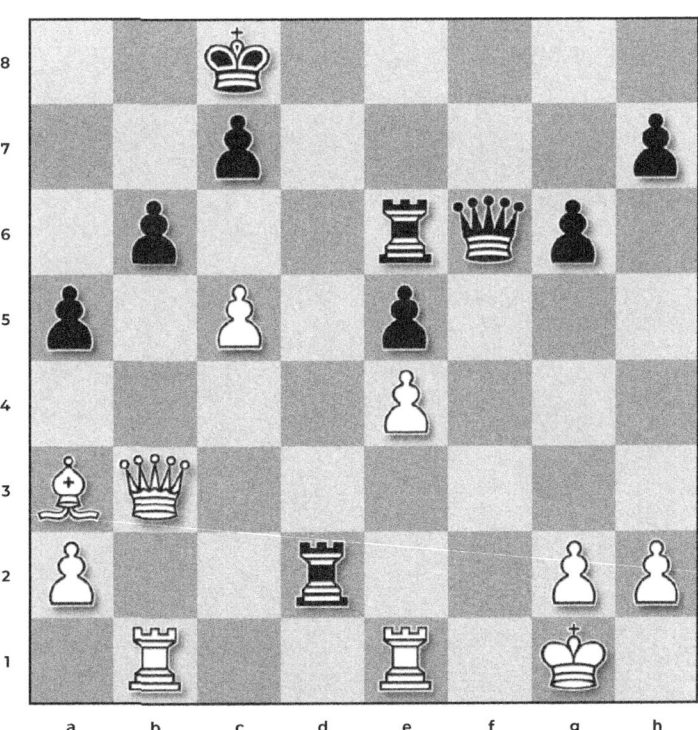

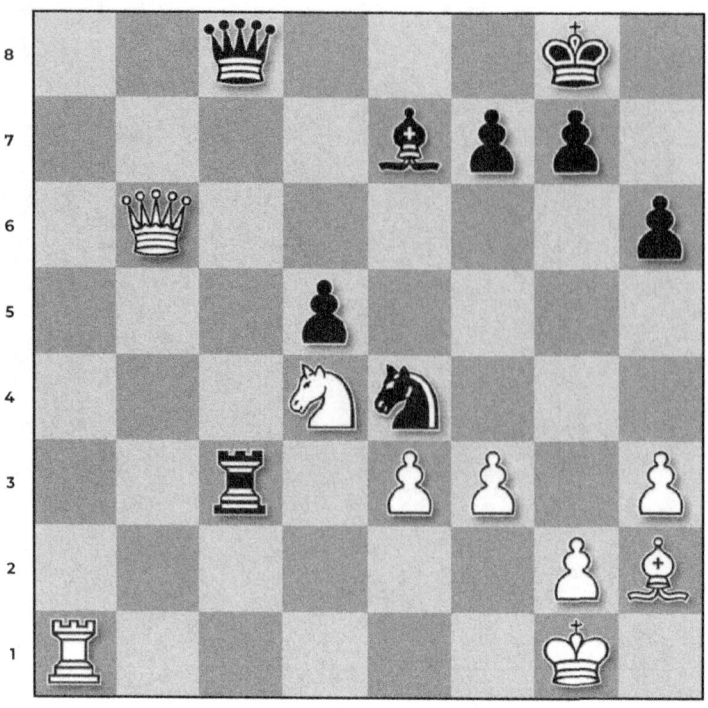

Puzzle 75

Black to move

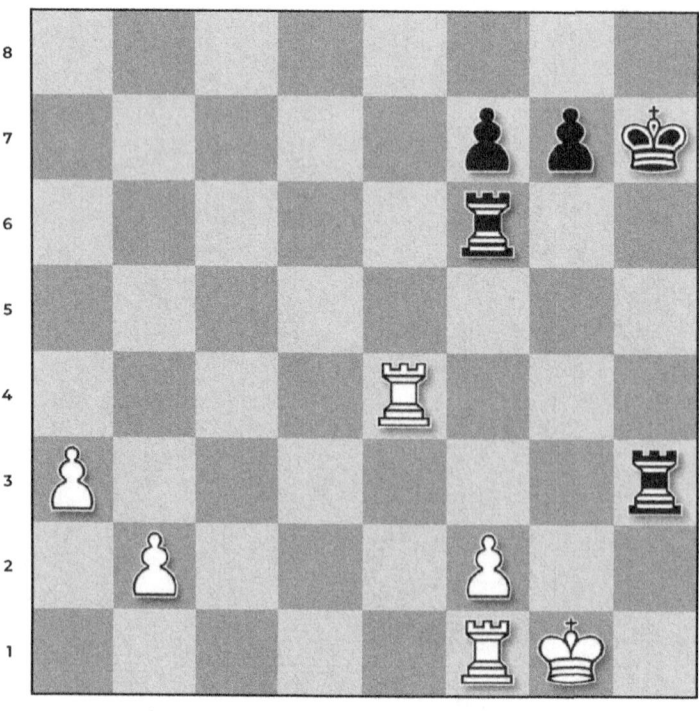

Puzzle 76

Black to move

Puzzle 77
Black to move

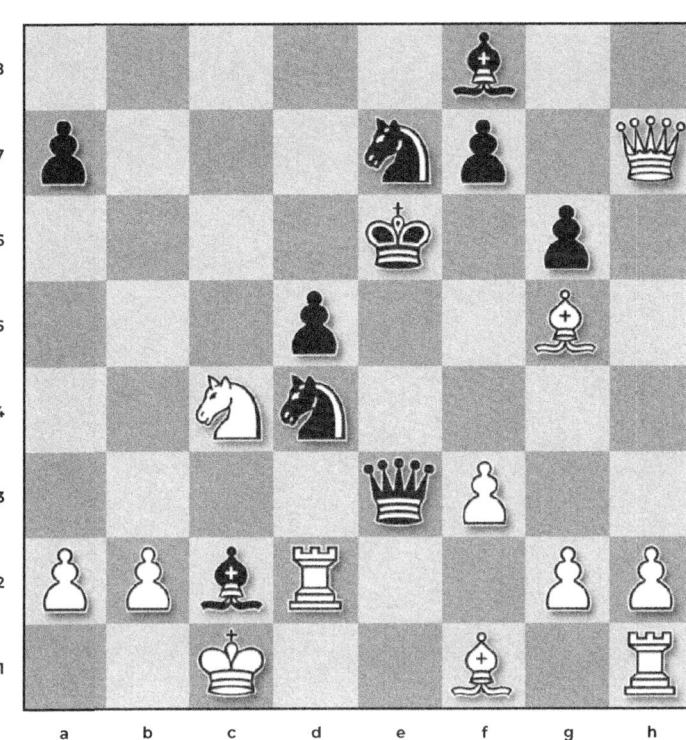

Puzzle 78
Black to move

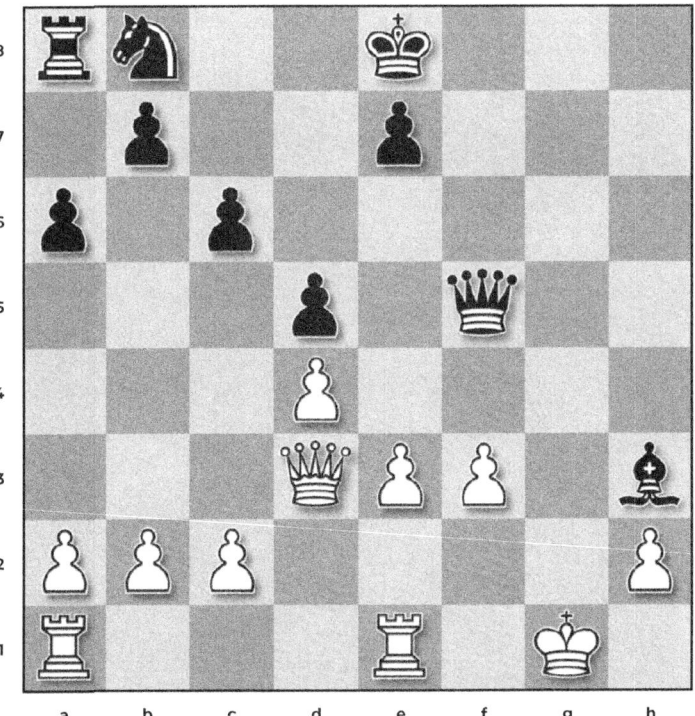

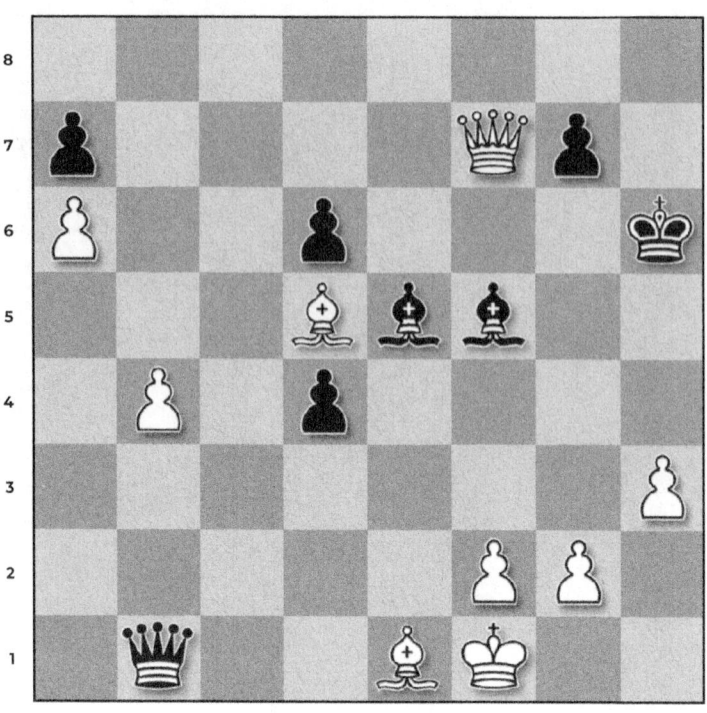

Puzzle 79
Black to move

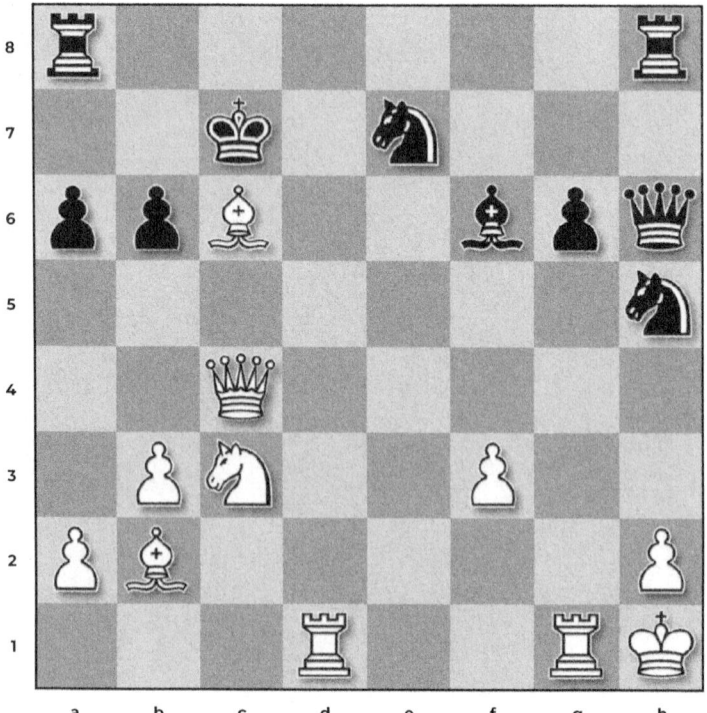

Puzzle 80
Black to move

Puzzle 81

Black to move

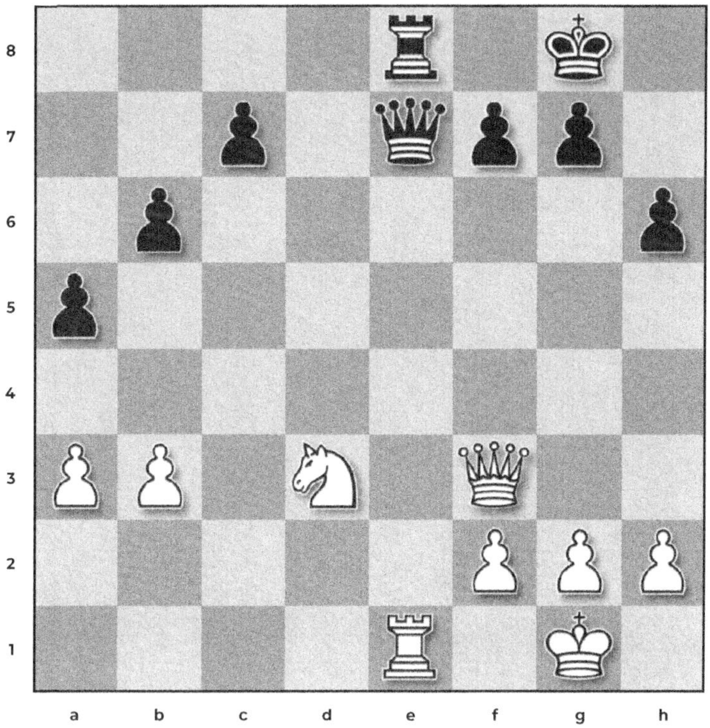

Puzzle 82

Black to move

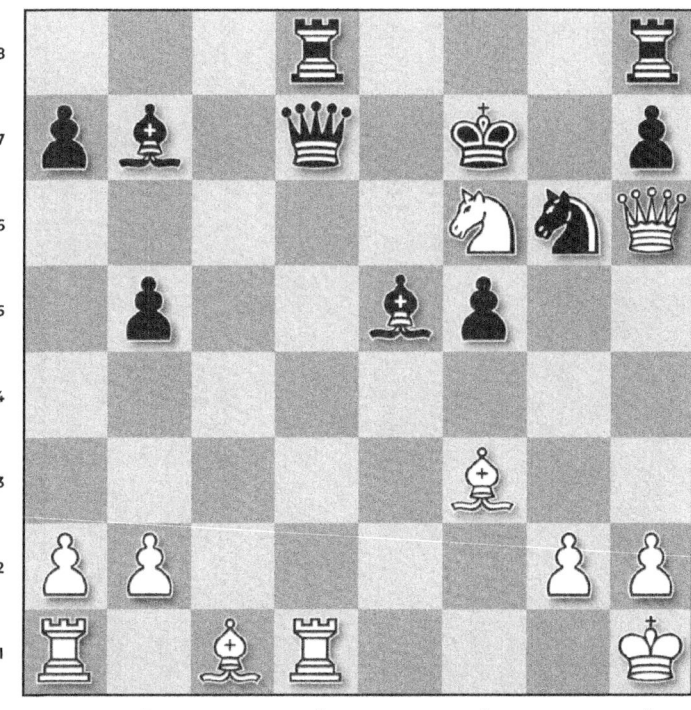

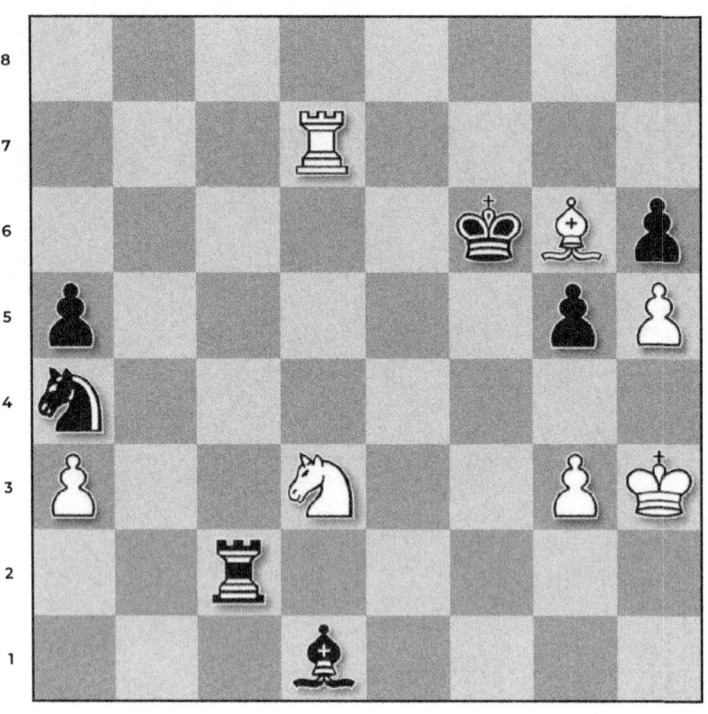

Puzzle 83
Black to move

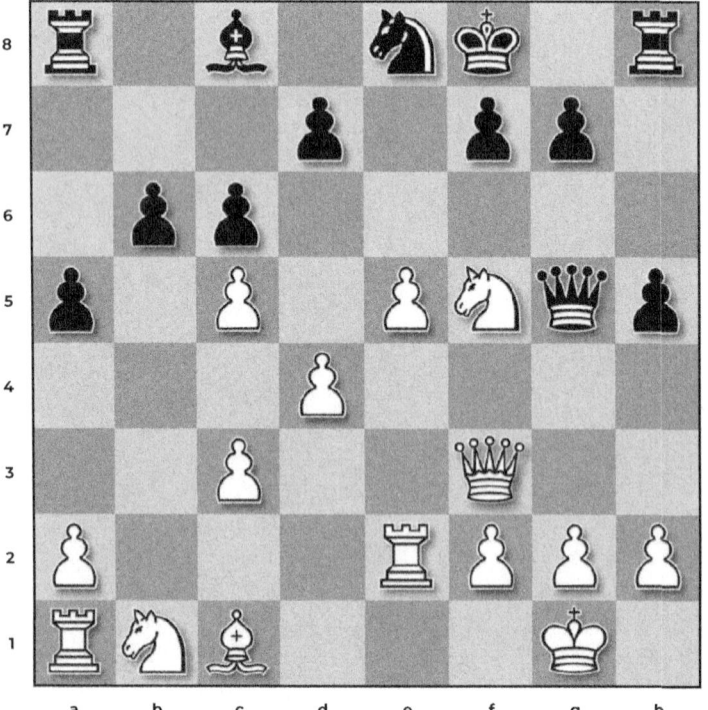

Puzzle 84
Black to move

Puzzle 85

Black to move

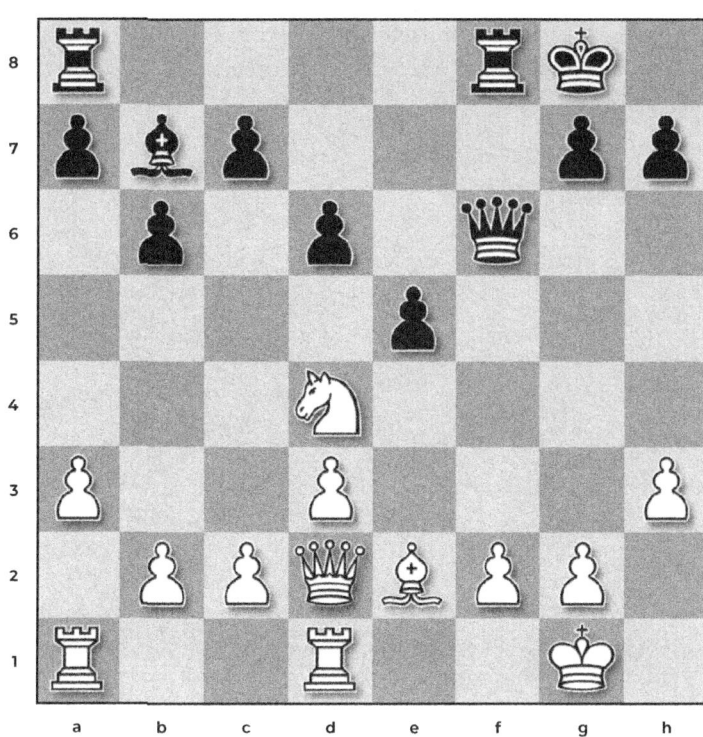

Puzzle 86

Black to move

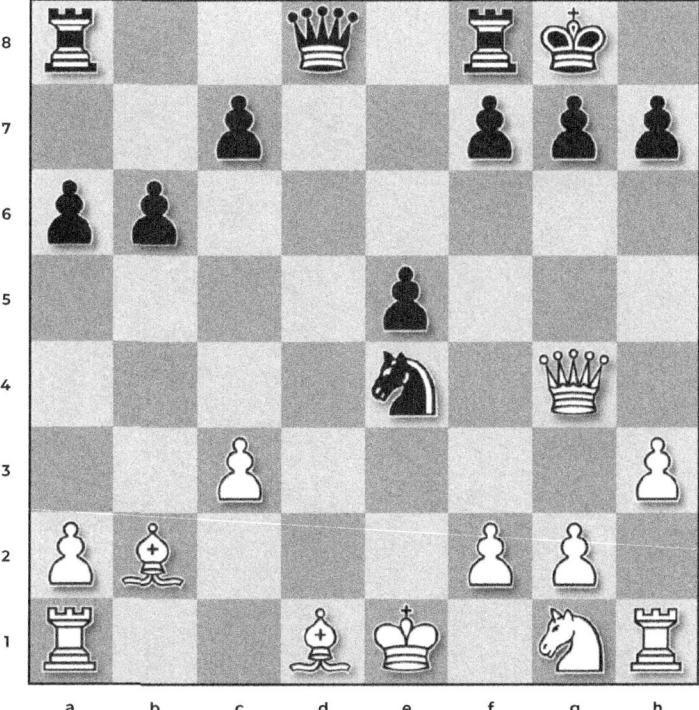

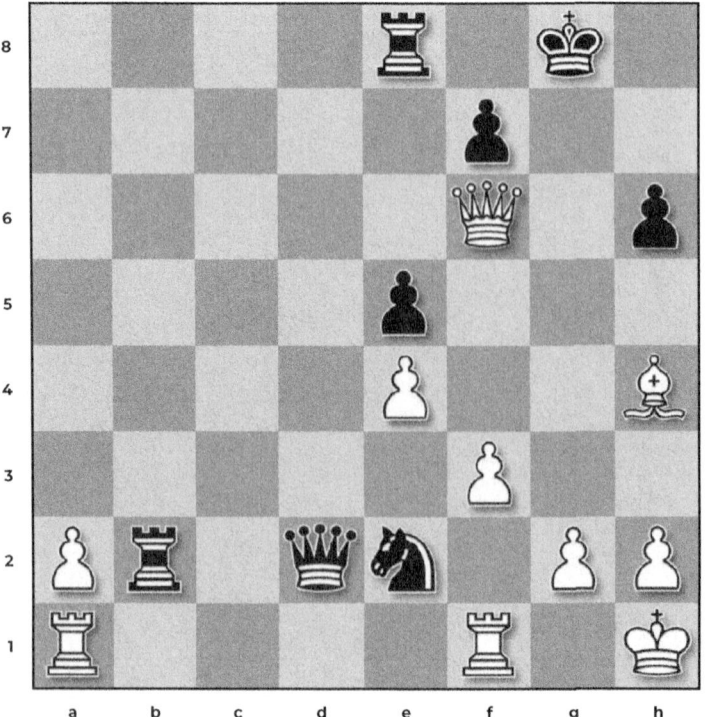

Puzzle 87

Black to move

Puzzle 88

Black to move

Puzzle 89
Black to move

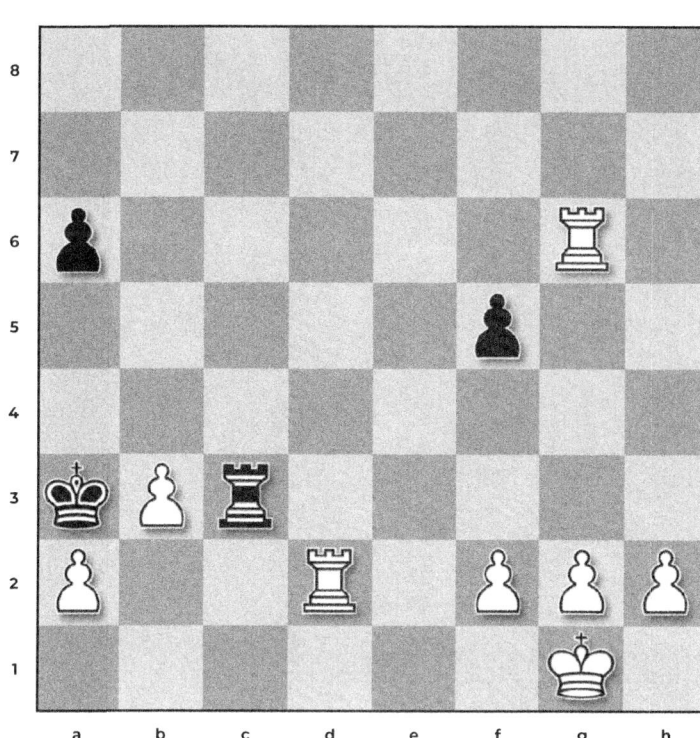

Puzzle 90
Black to move

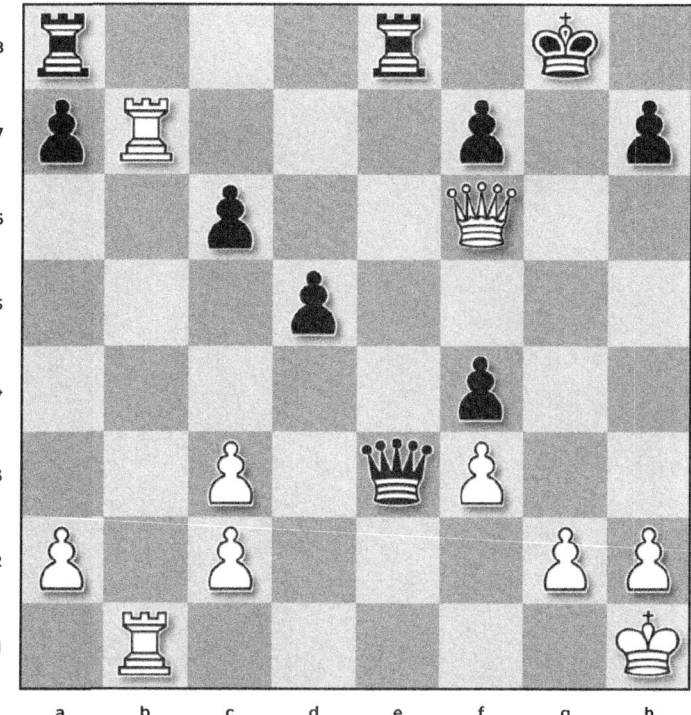

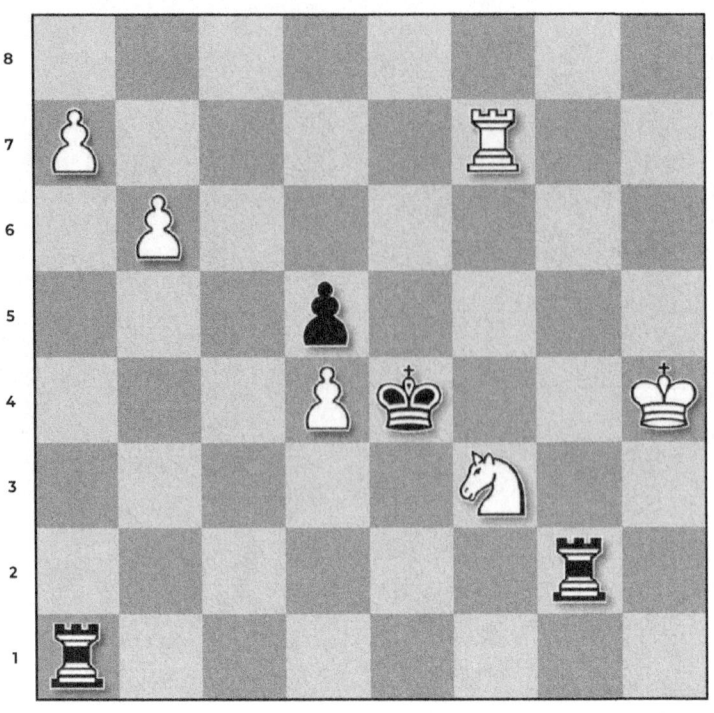

Puzzle 91
Black to move

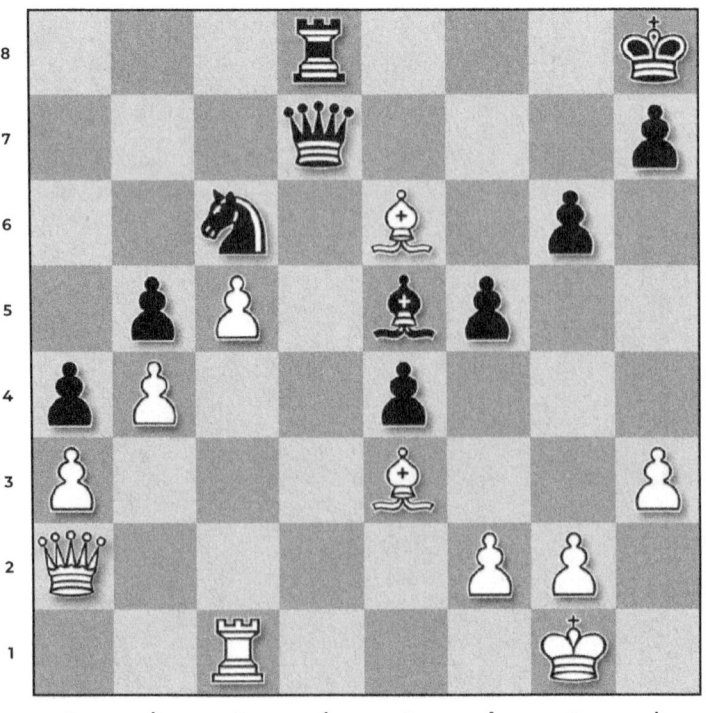

Puzzle 92
Black to move

Puzzle 93

Black to move

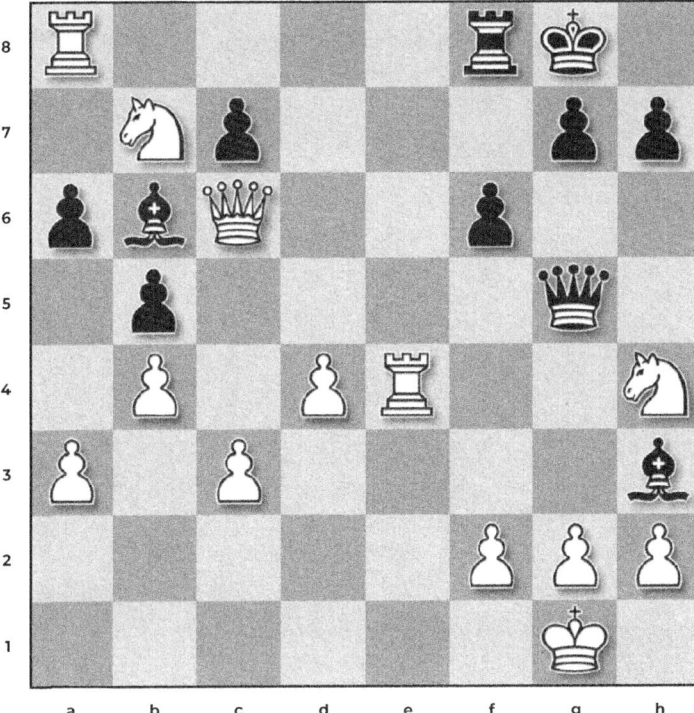

Puzzle 94

Black to move

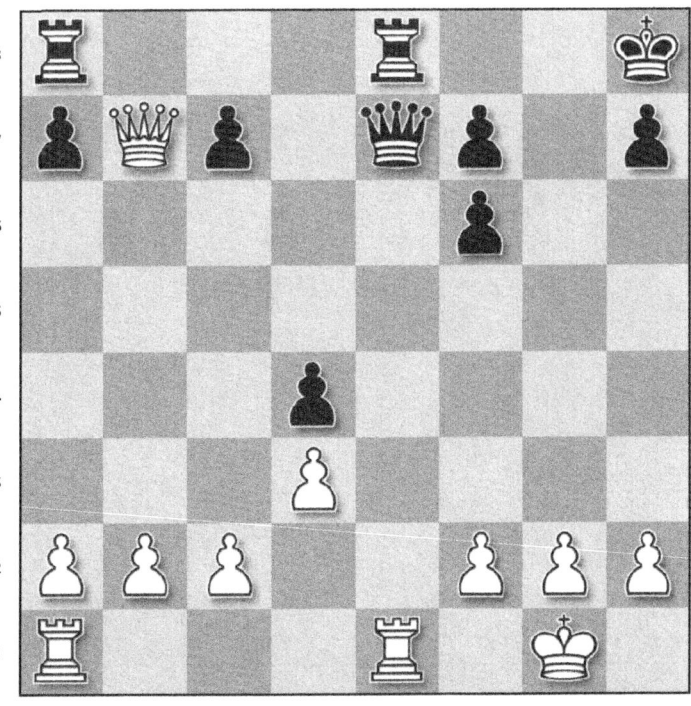

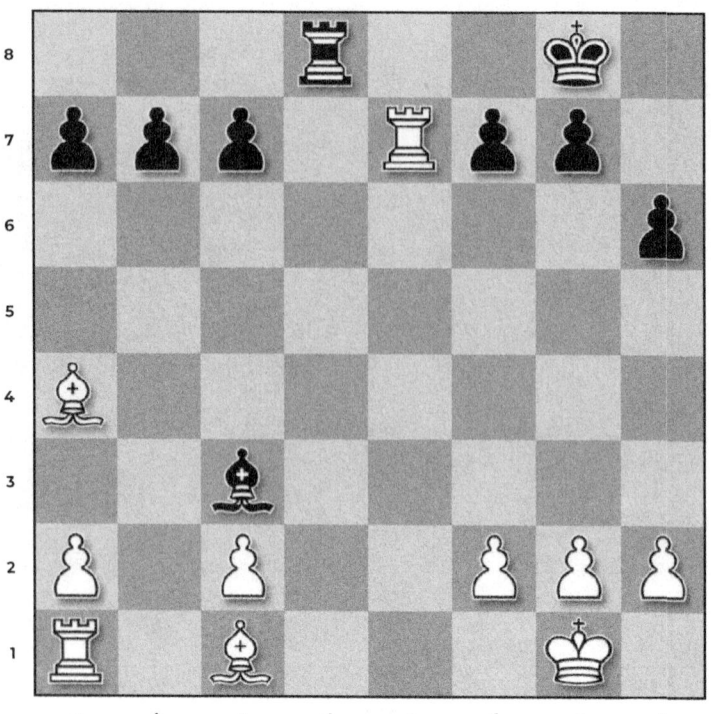

Puzzle 95
Black to move

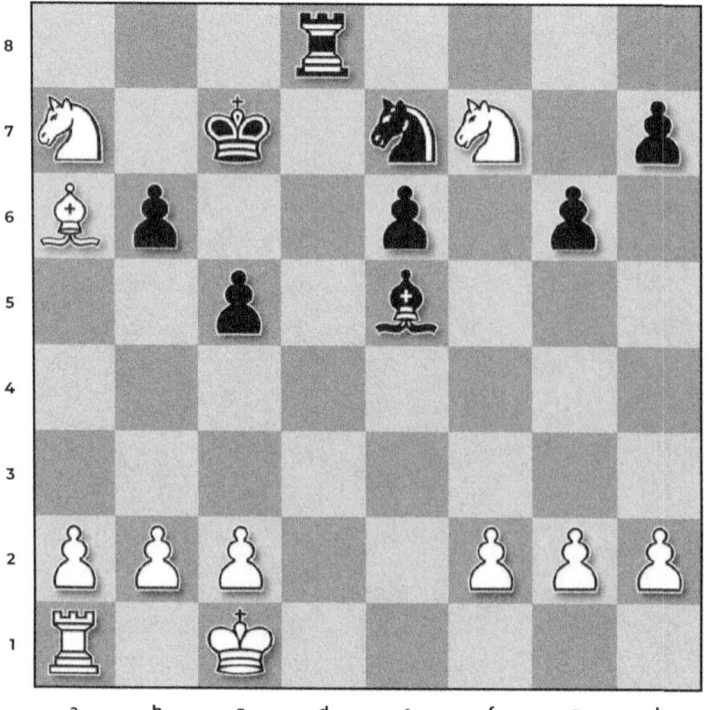

Puzzle 96
Black to move

Puzzle 97

Black to move

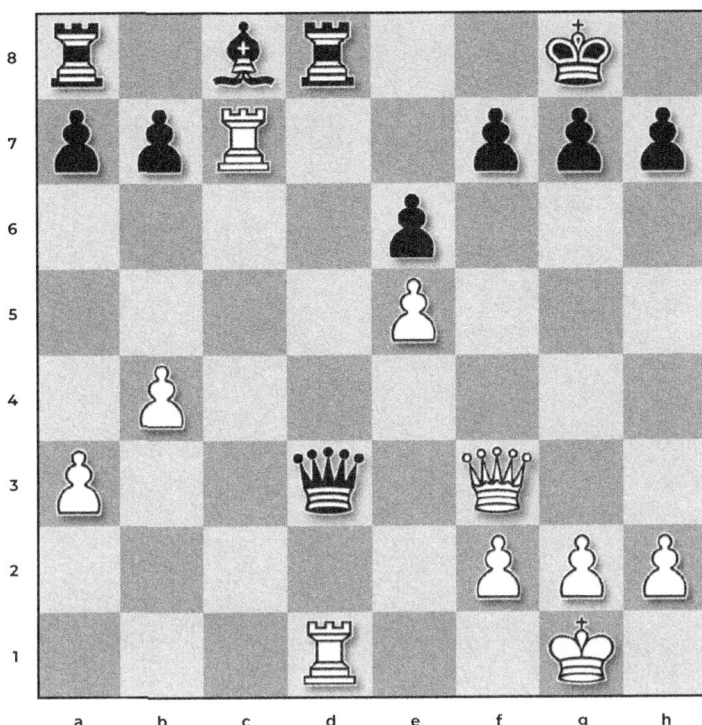

Puzzle 98

Black to move

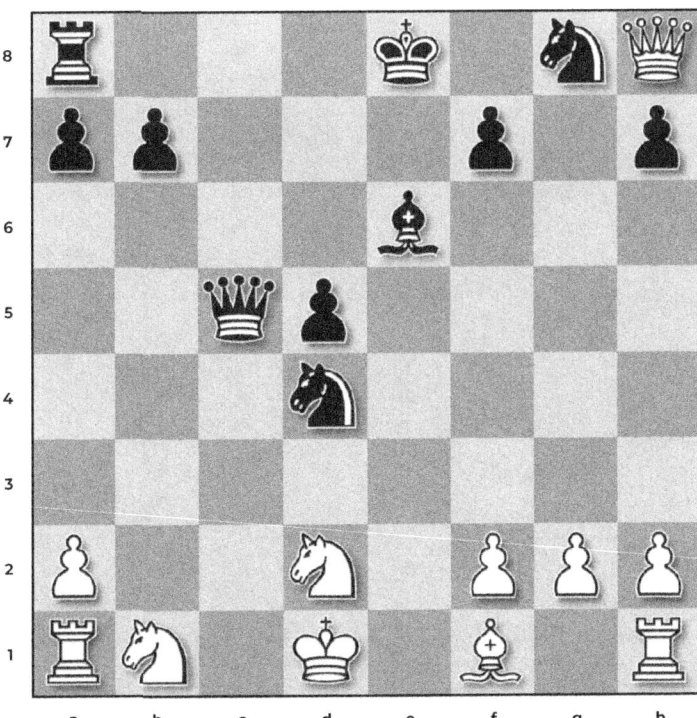

Puzzle 99
Black to move

Puzzle 100
Black to move

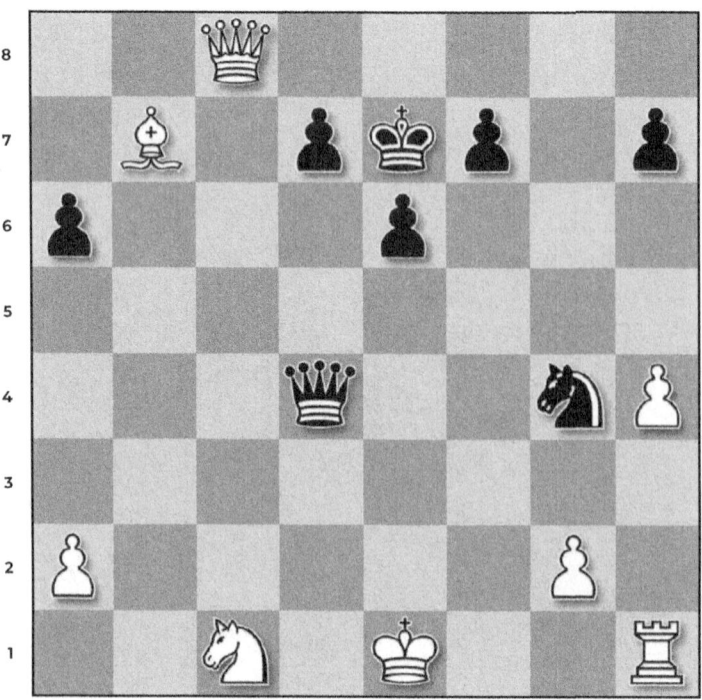

SOLUTIONS

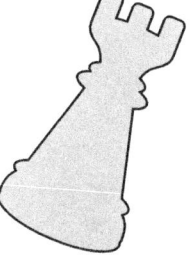

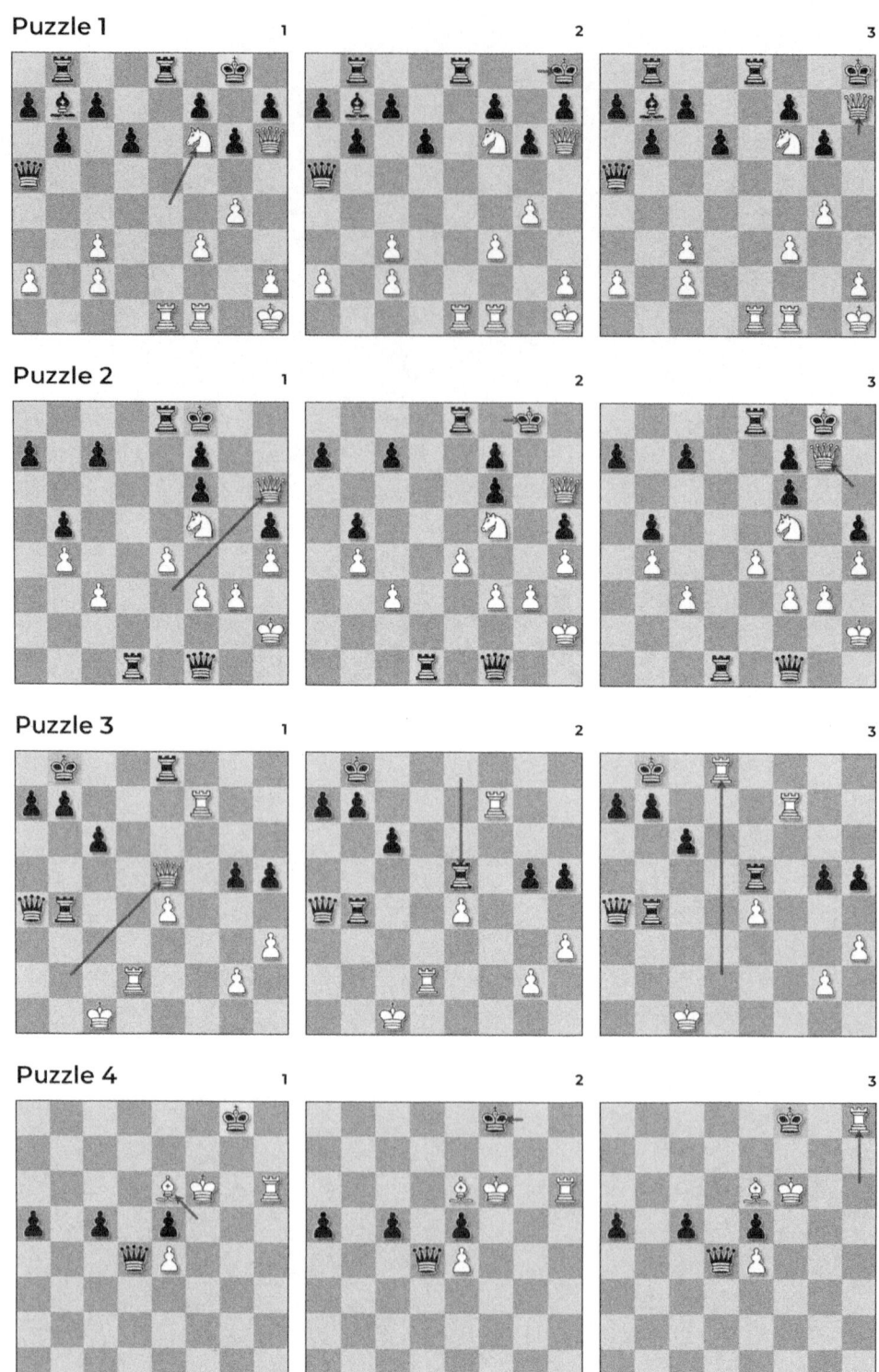

SOLUTIONS

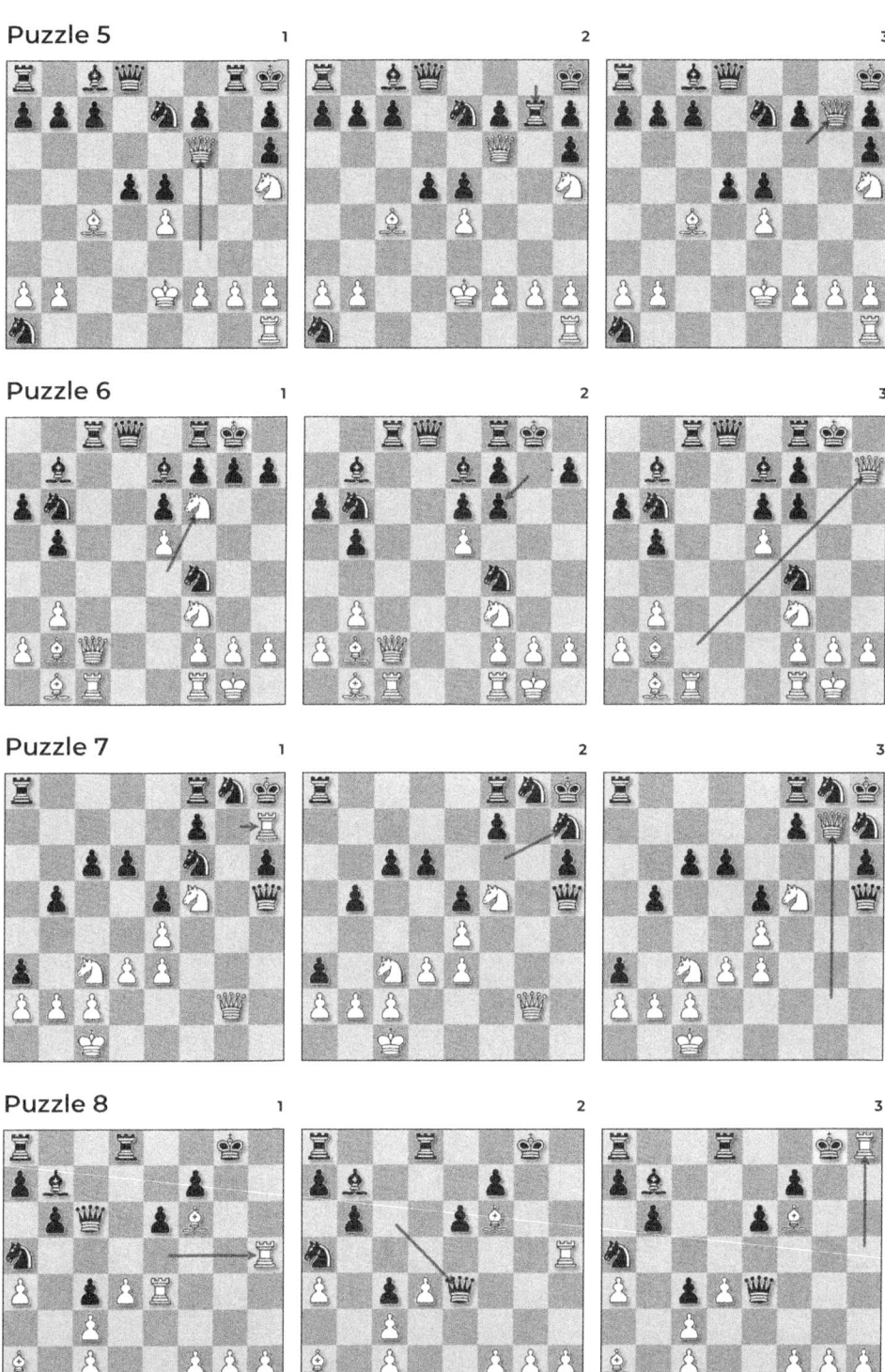

SOLUTIONS

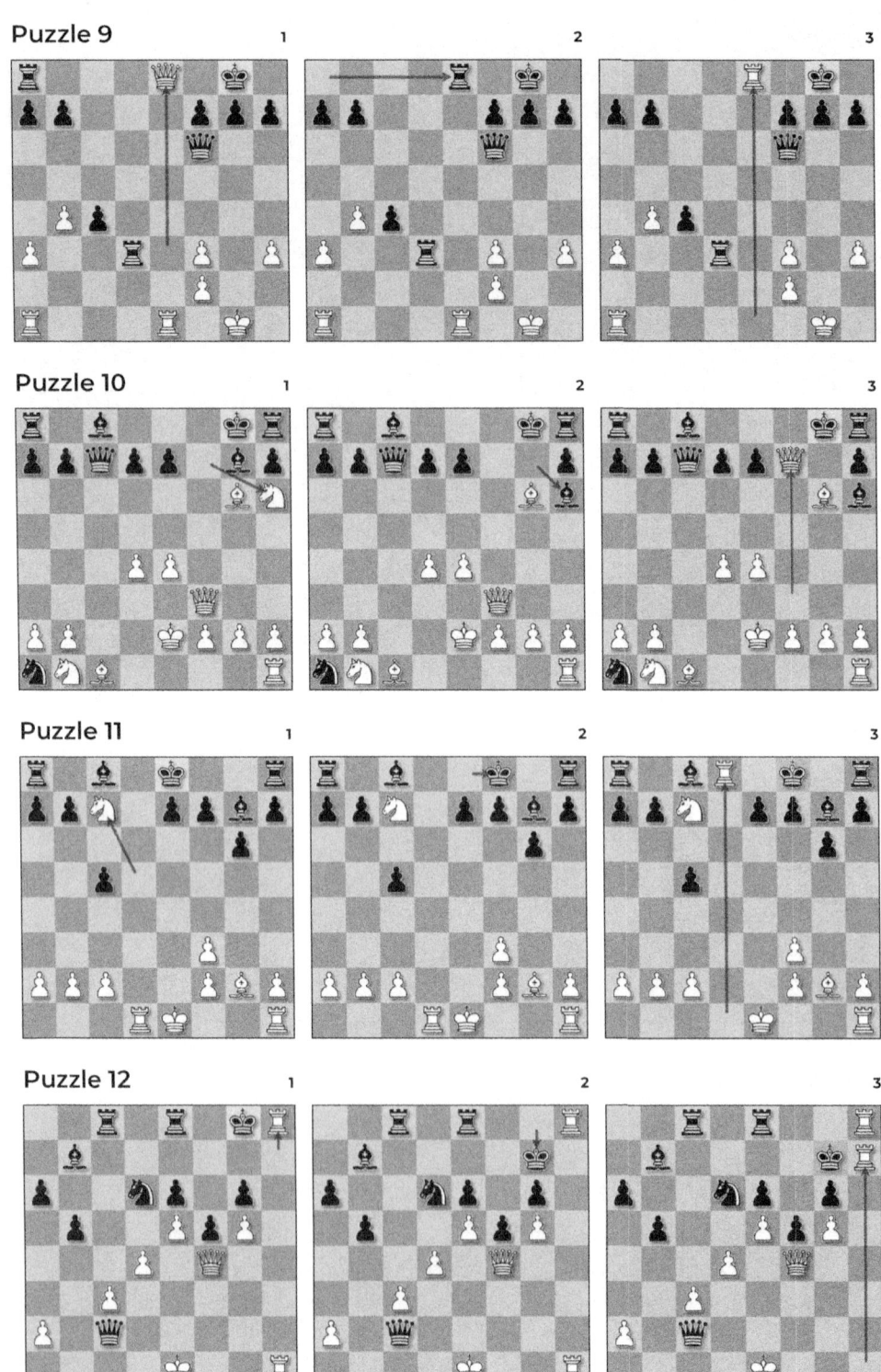

Puzzle 9

Puzzle 10

Puzzle 11

Puzzle 12

SOLUTIONS

Puzzle 13

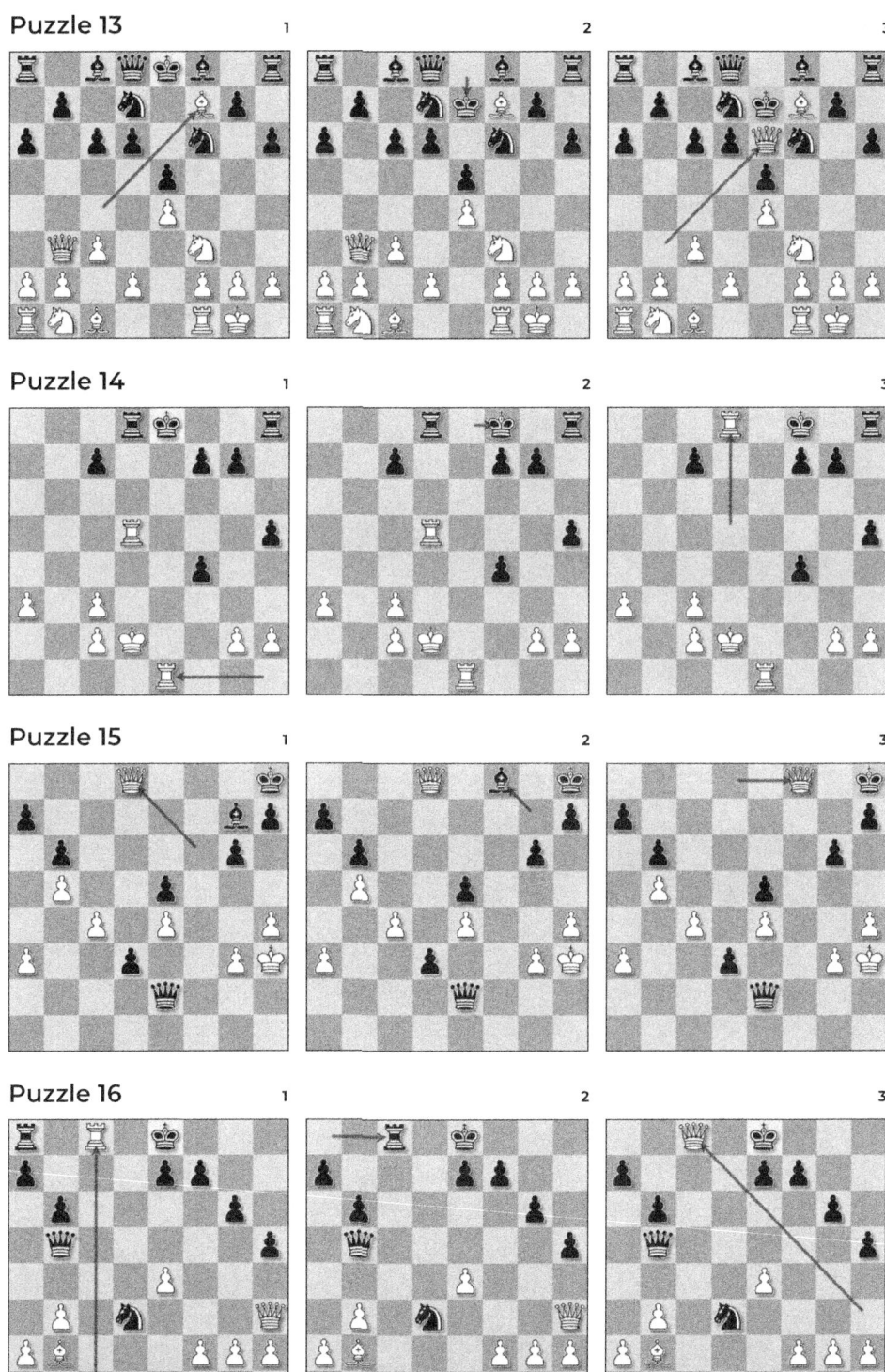

Puzzle 14

Puzzle 15

Puzzle 16

SOLUTIONS

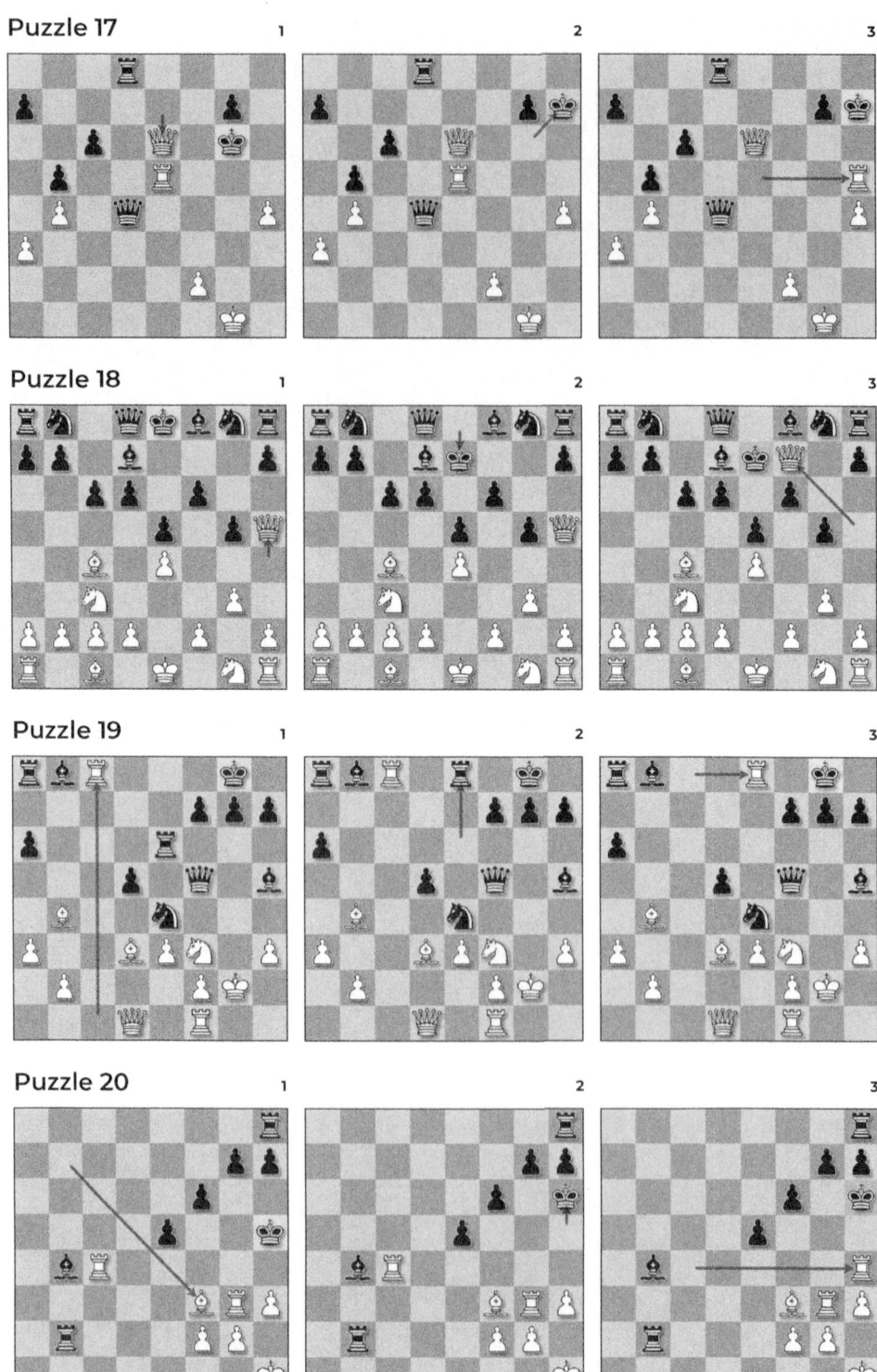

SOLUTIONS

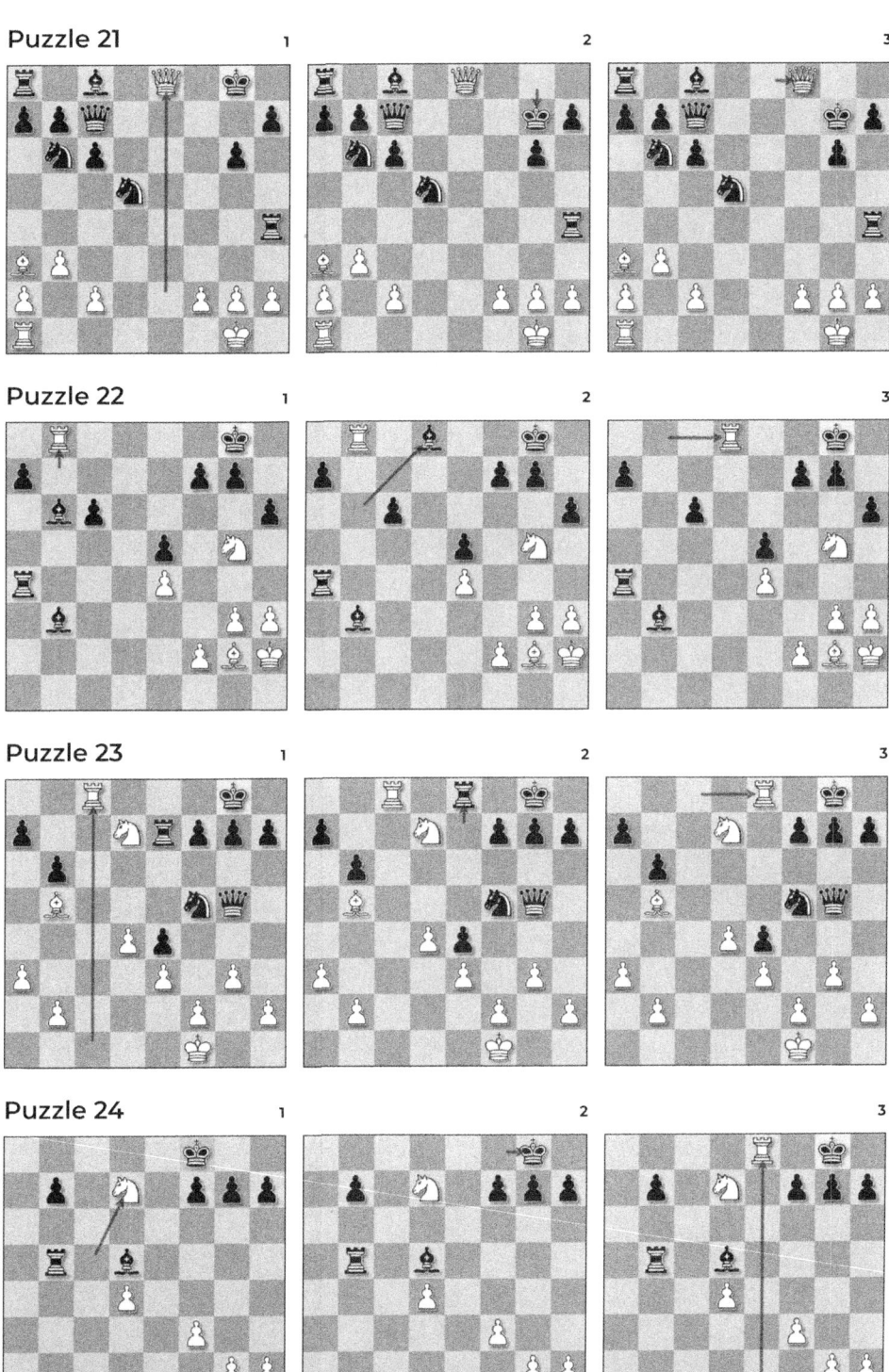

SOLUTIONS

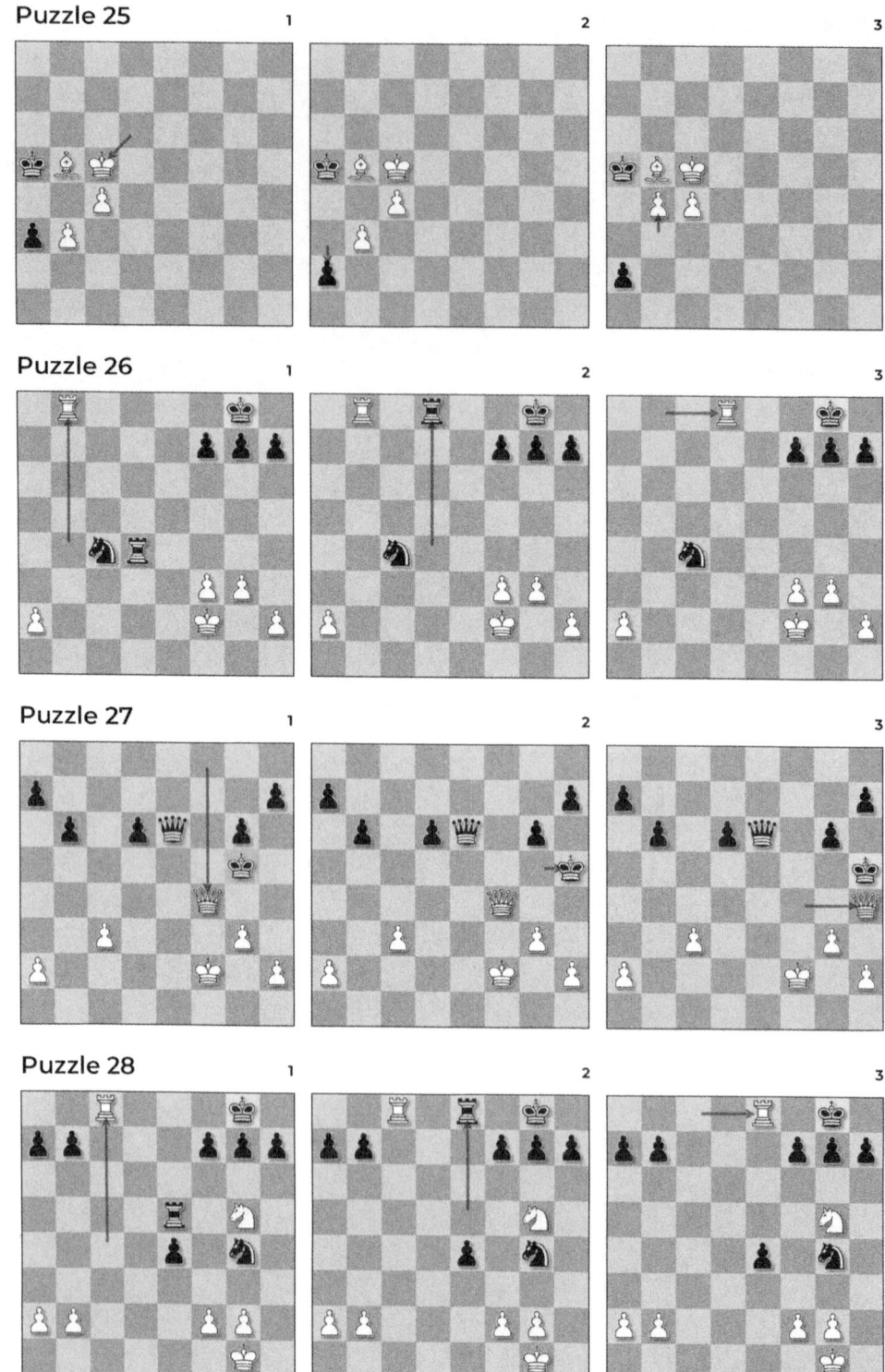

SOLUTIONS

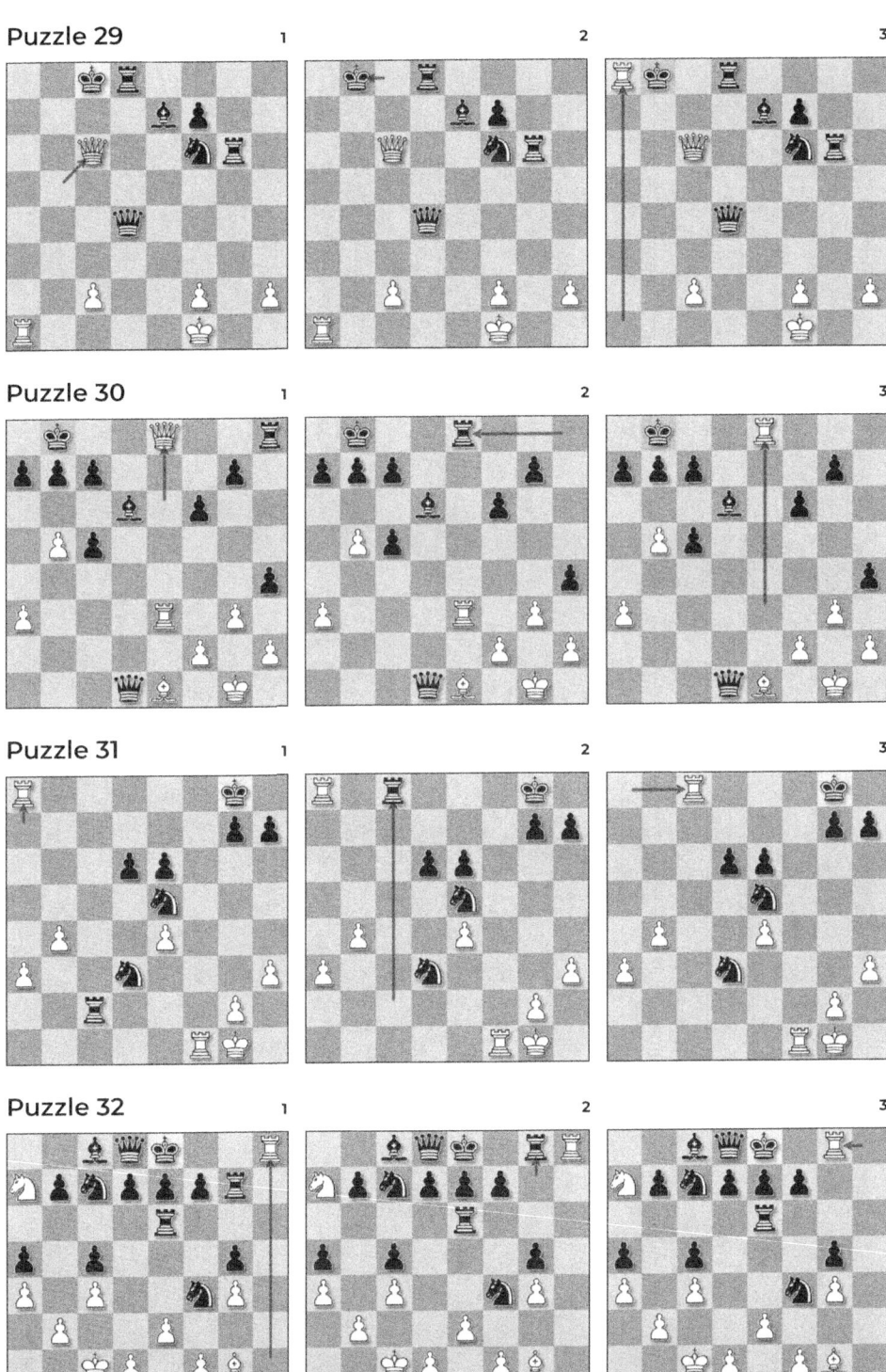

SOLUTIONS

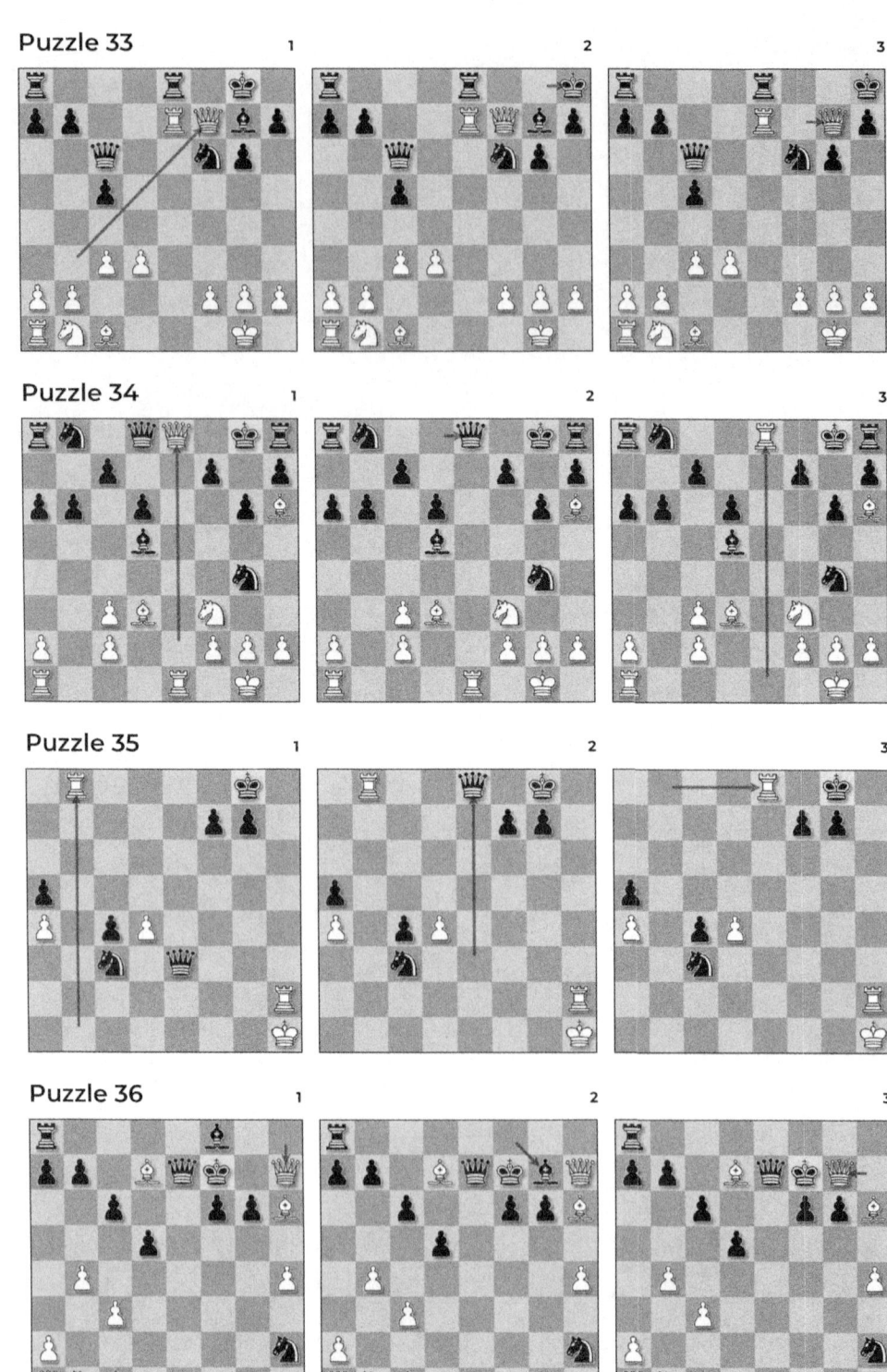

SOLUTIONS

Puzzle 37

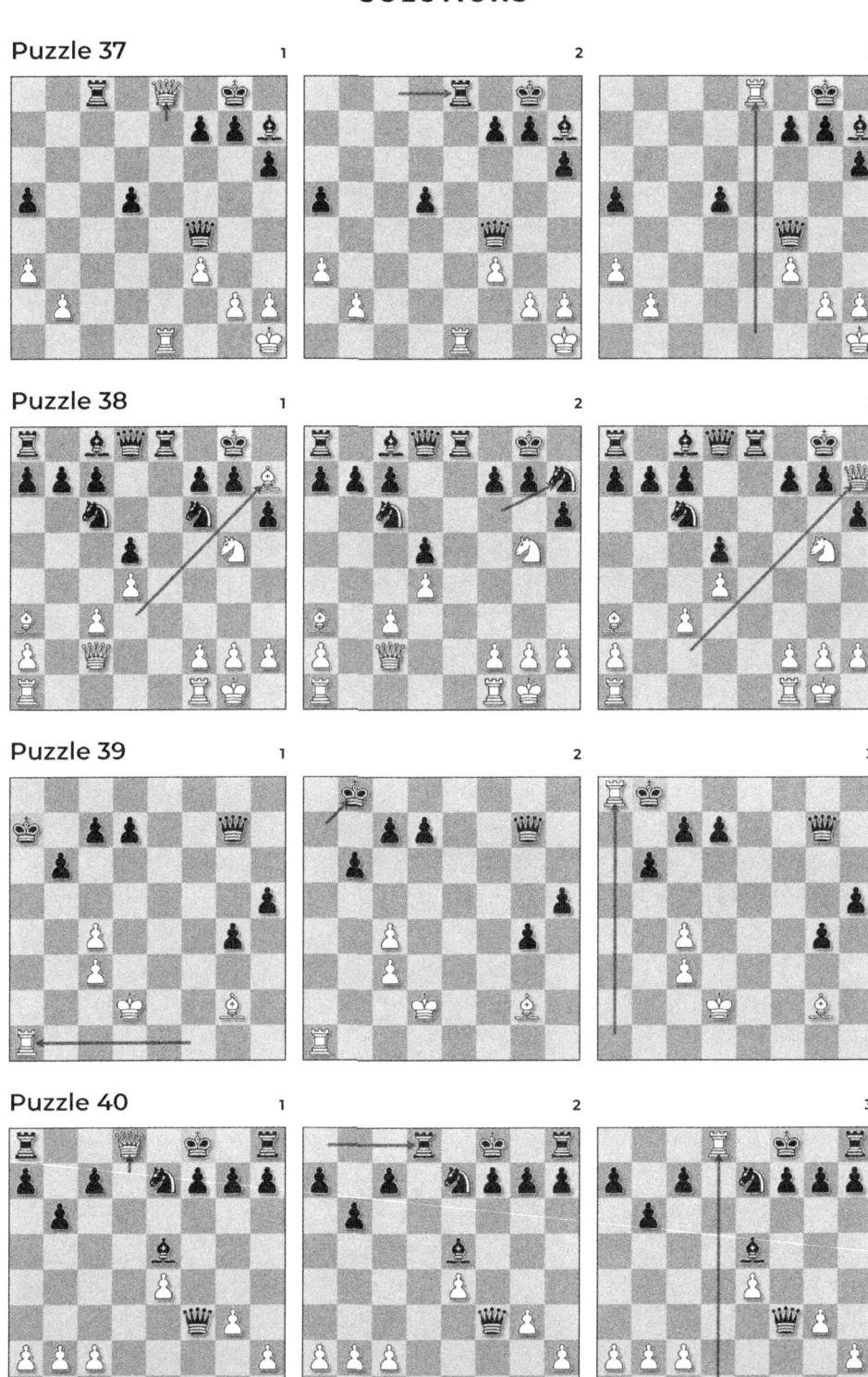

SOLUTIONS

Puzzle 41

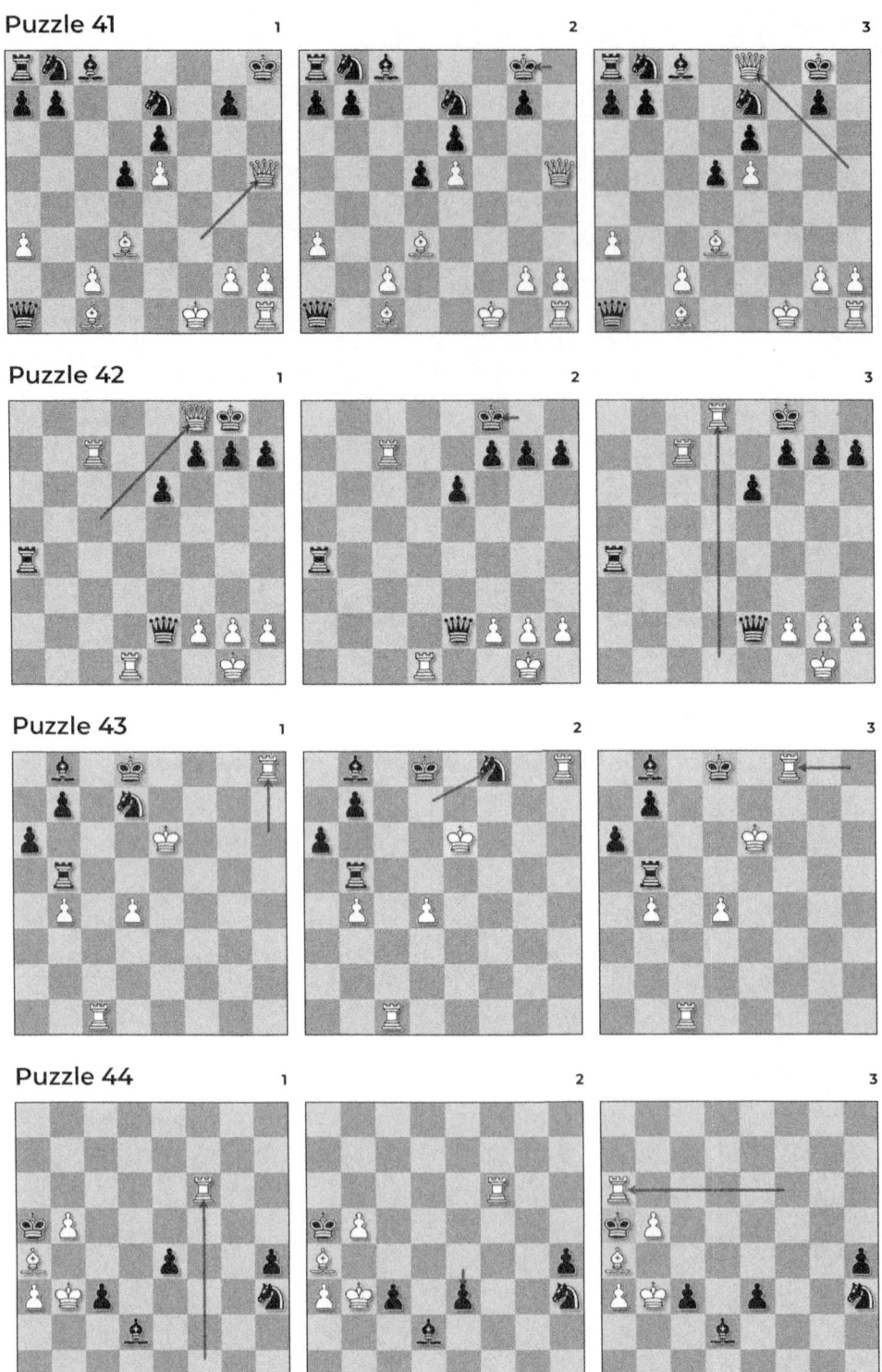

SOLUTIONS

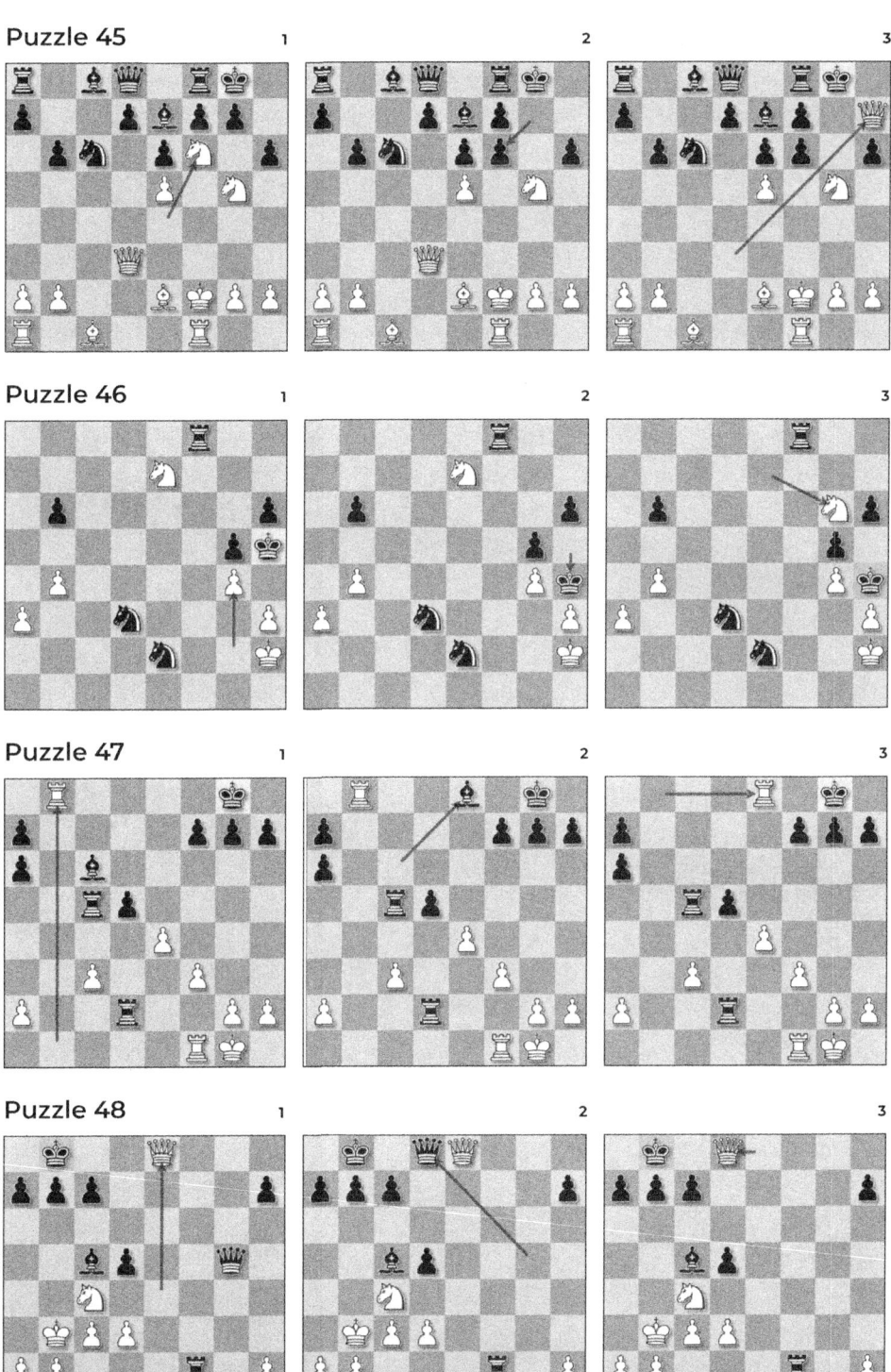

SOLUTIONS

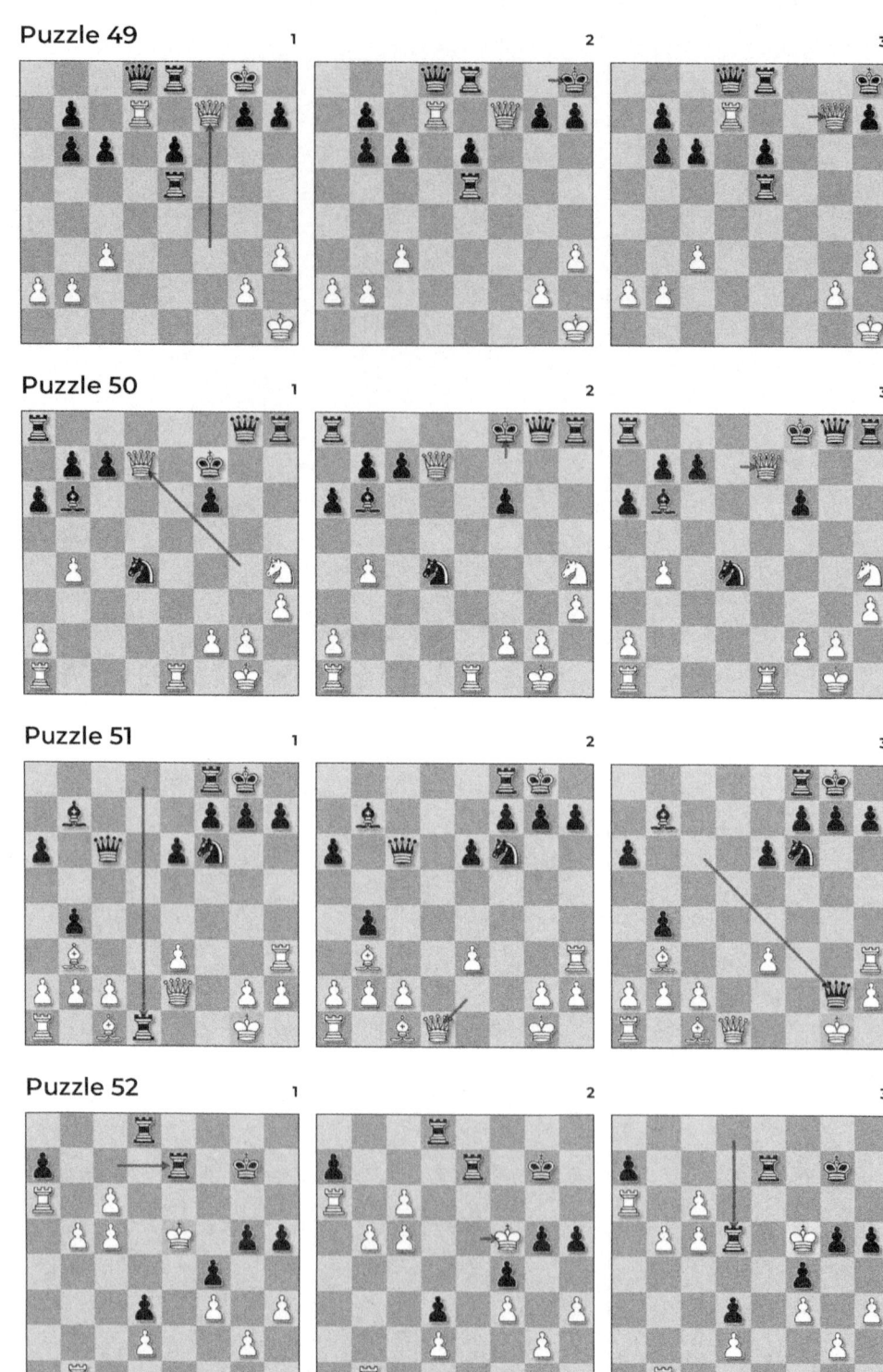

SOLUTIONS

Puzzle 53

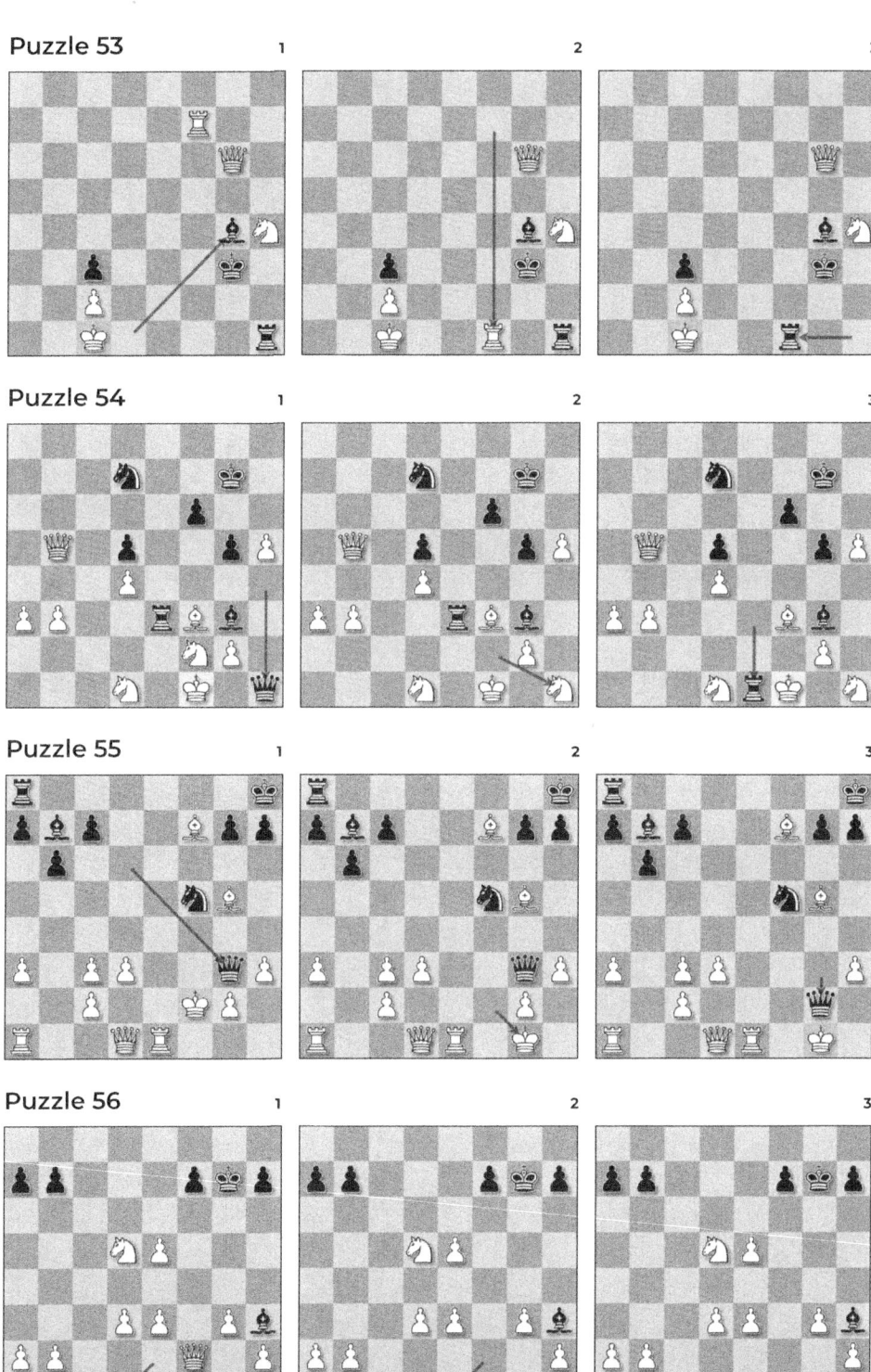

SOLUTIONS

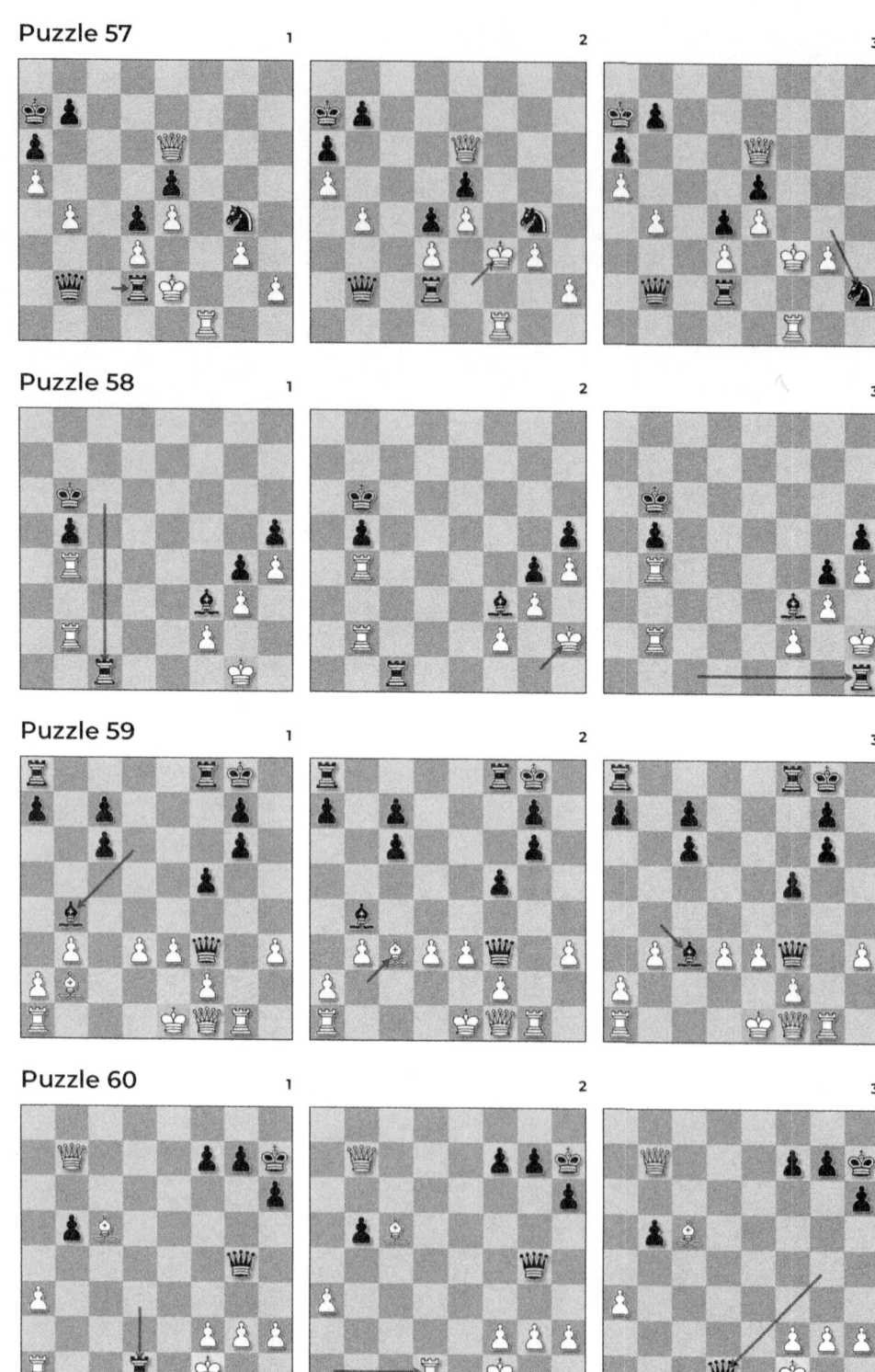

SOLUTIONS

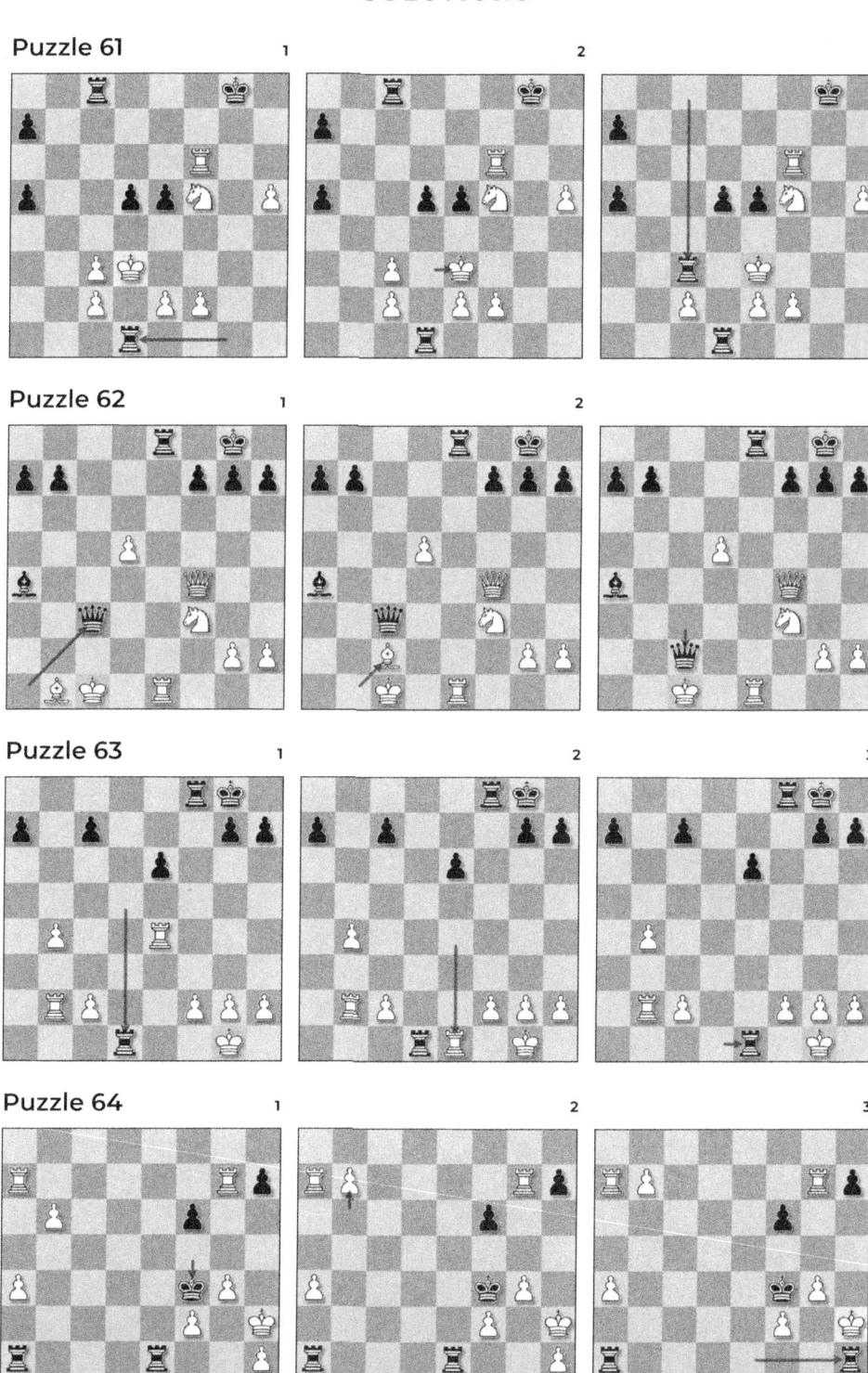

SOLUTIONS

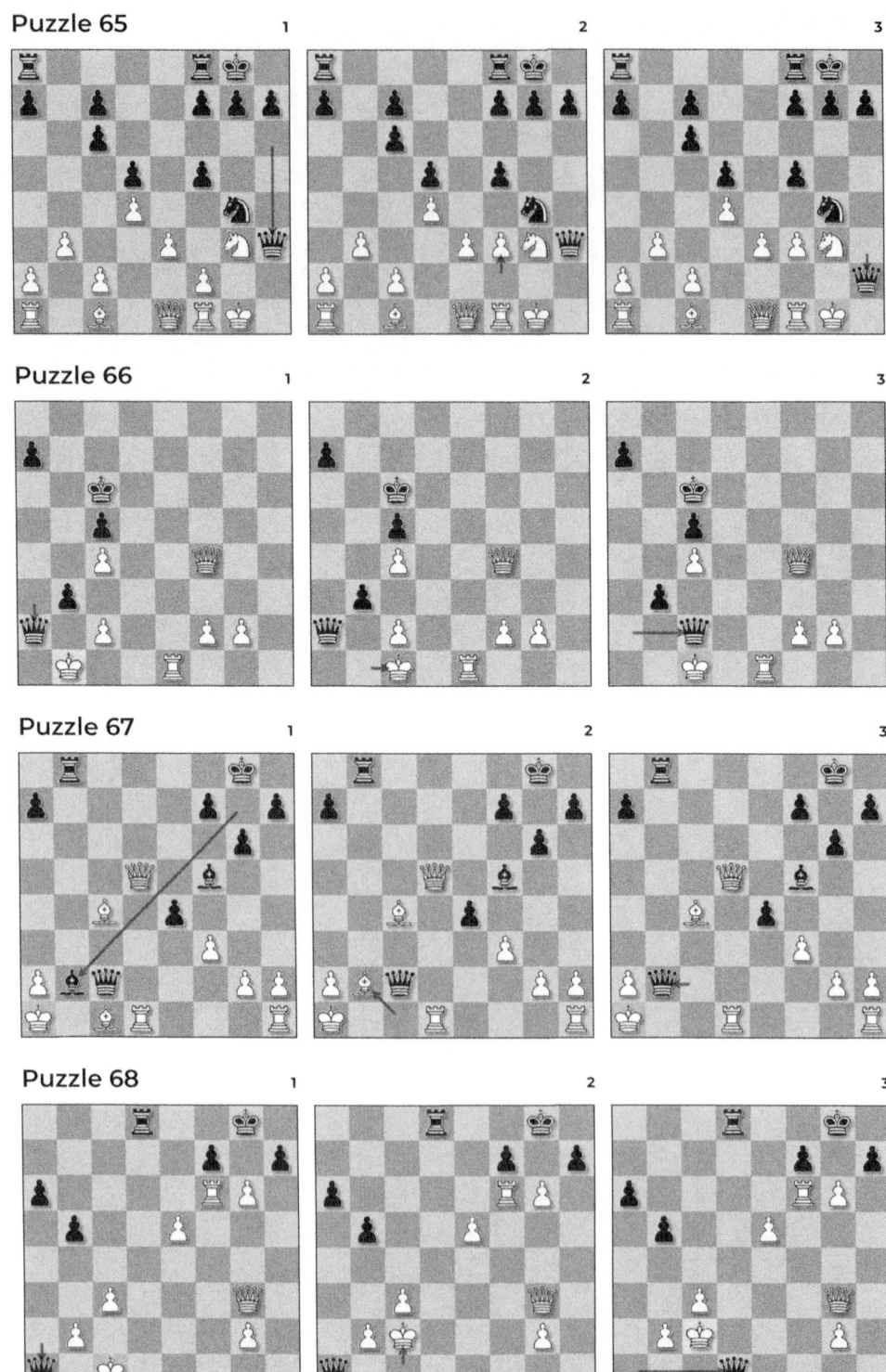

SOLUTIONS

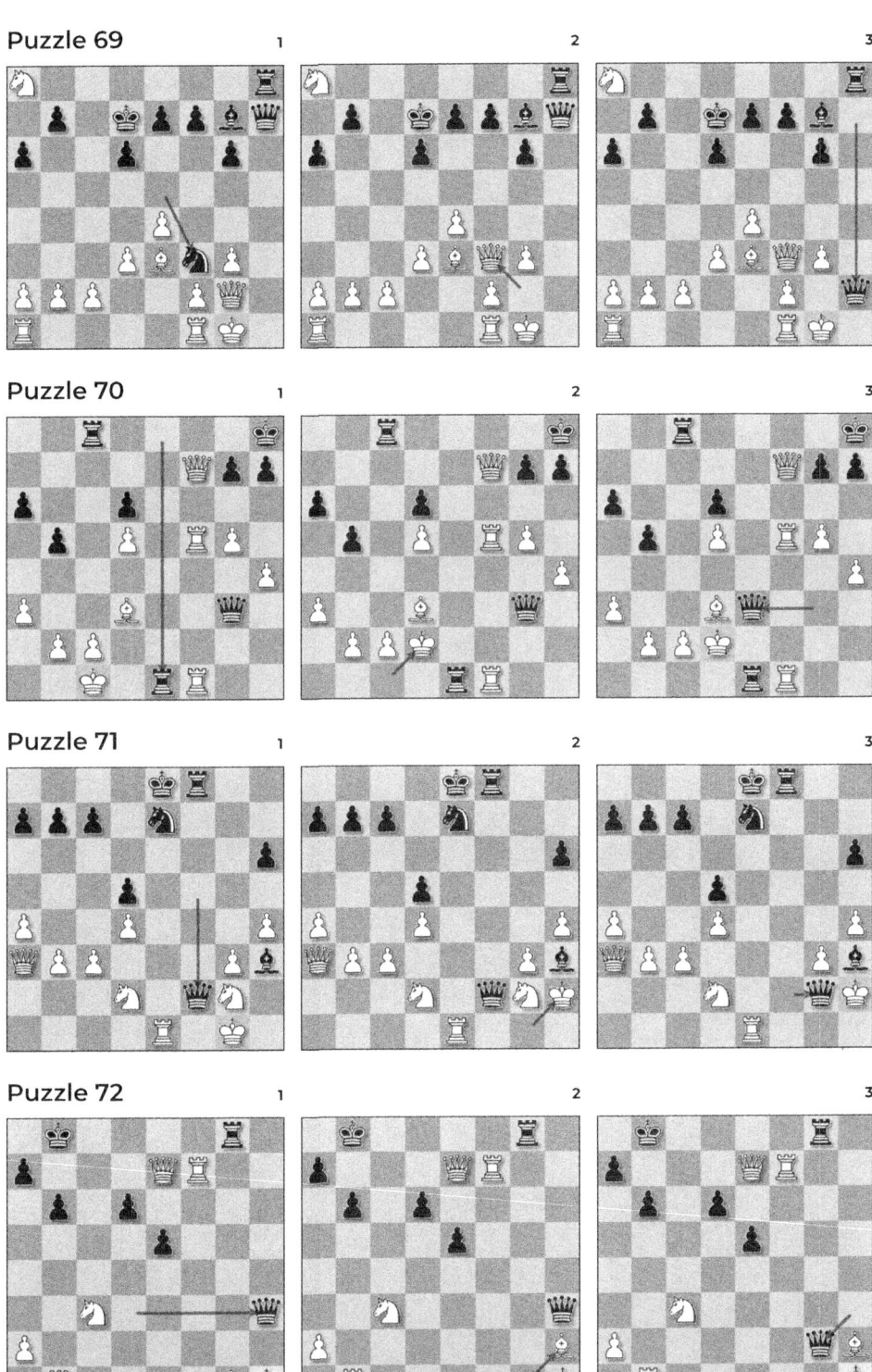

SOLUTIONS

Puzzle 73

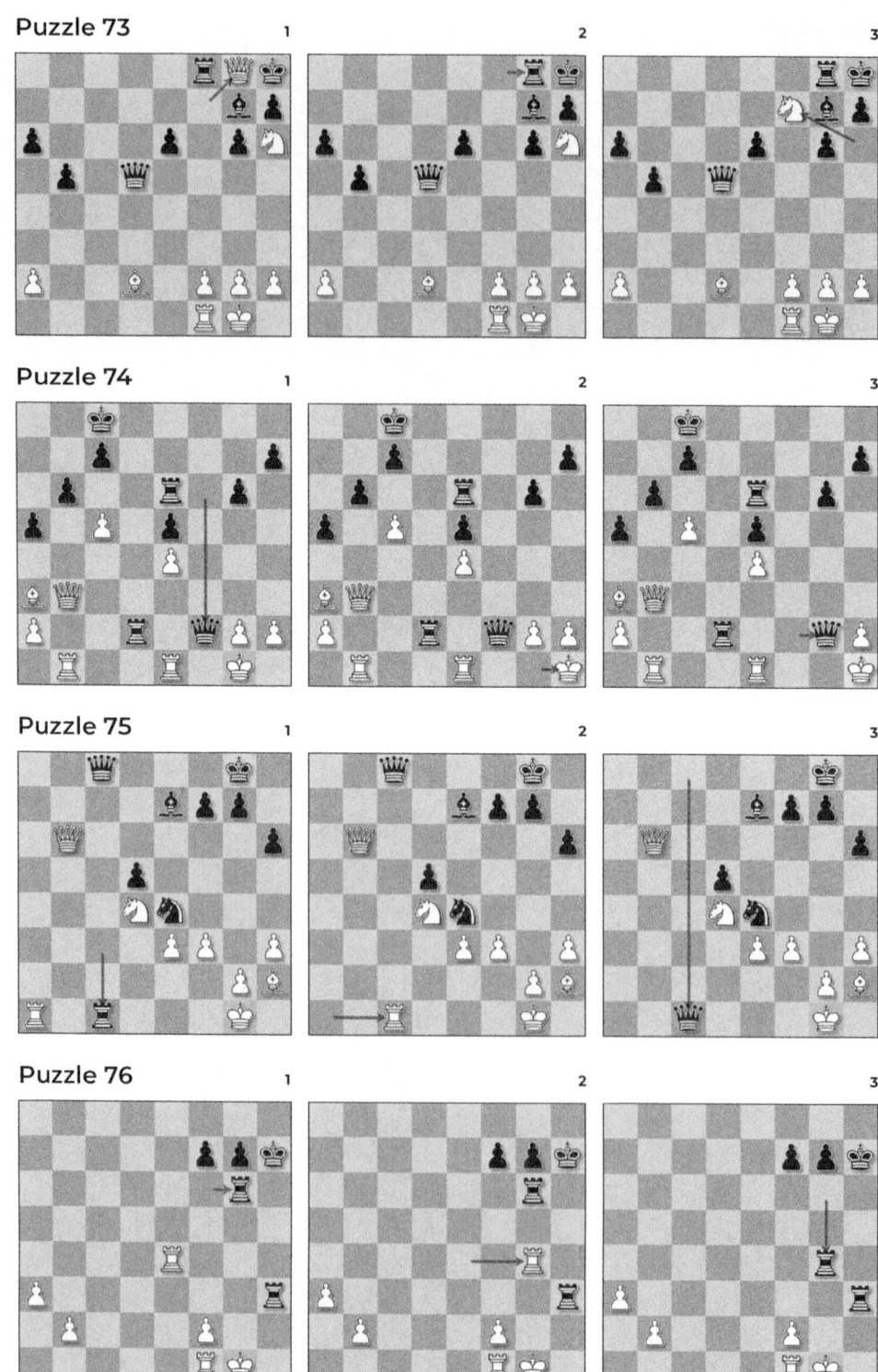

SOLUTIONS

Puzzle 77

Puzzle 78

Puzzle 79

Puzzle 80

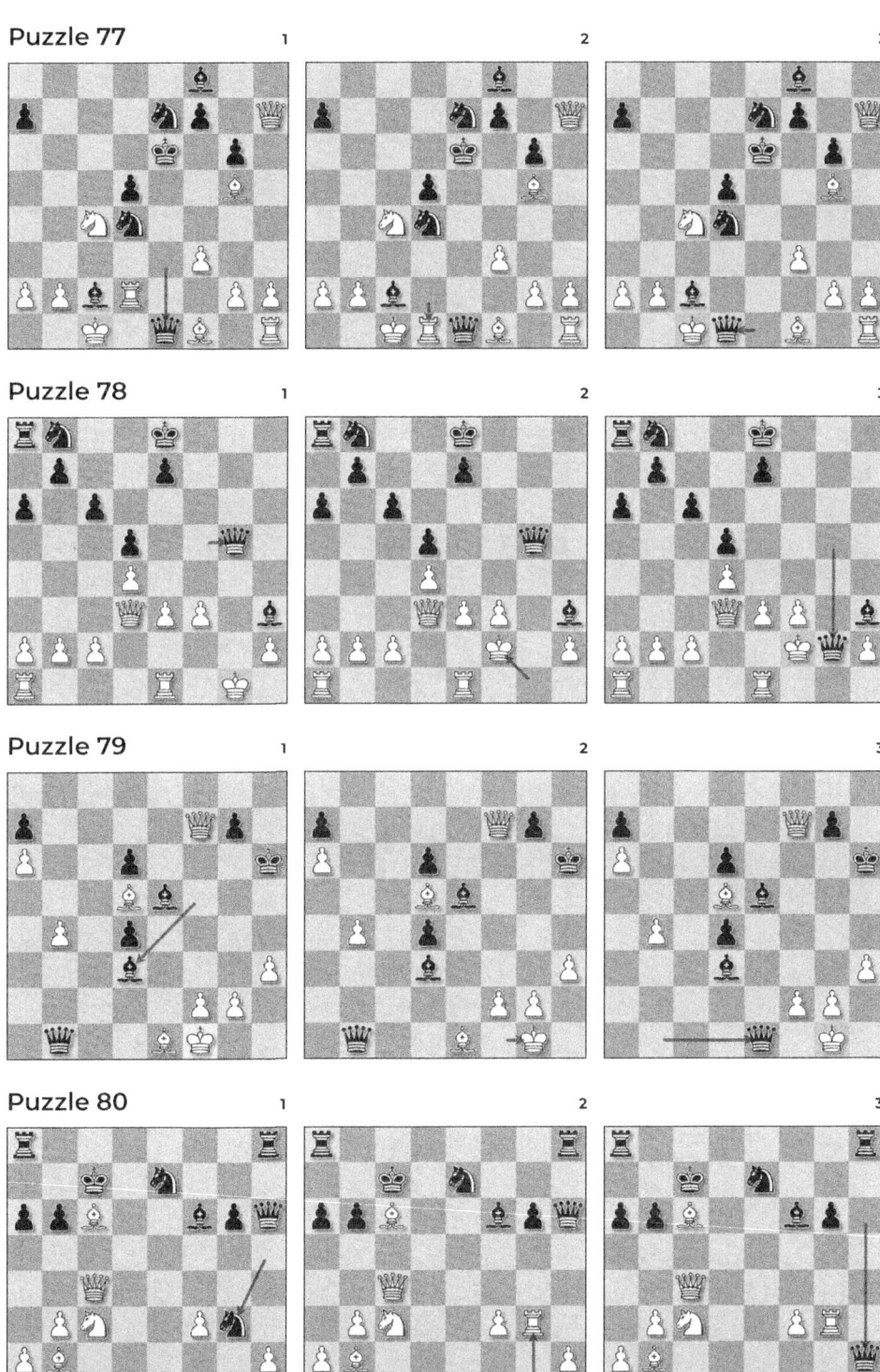

SOLUTIONS

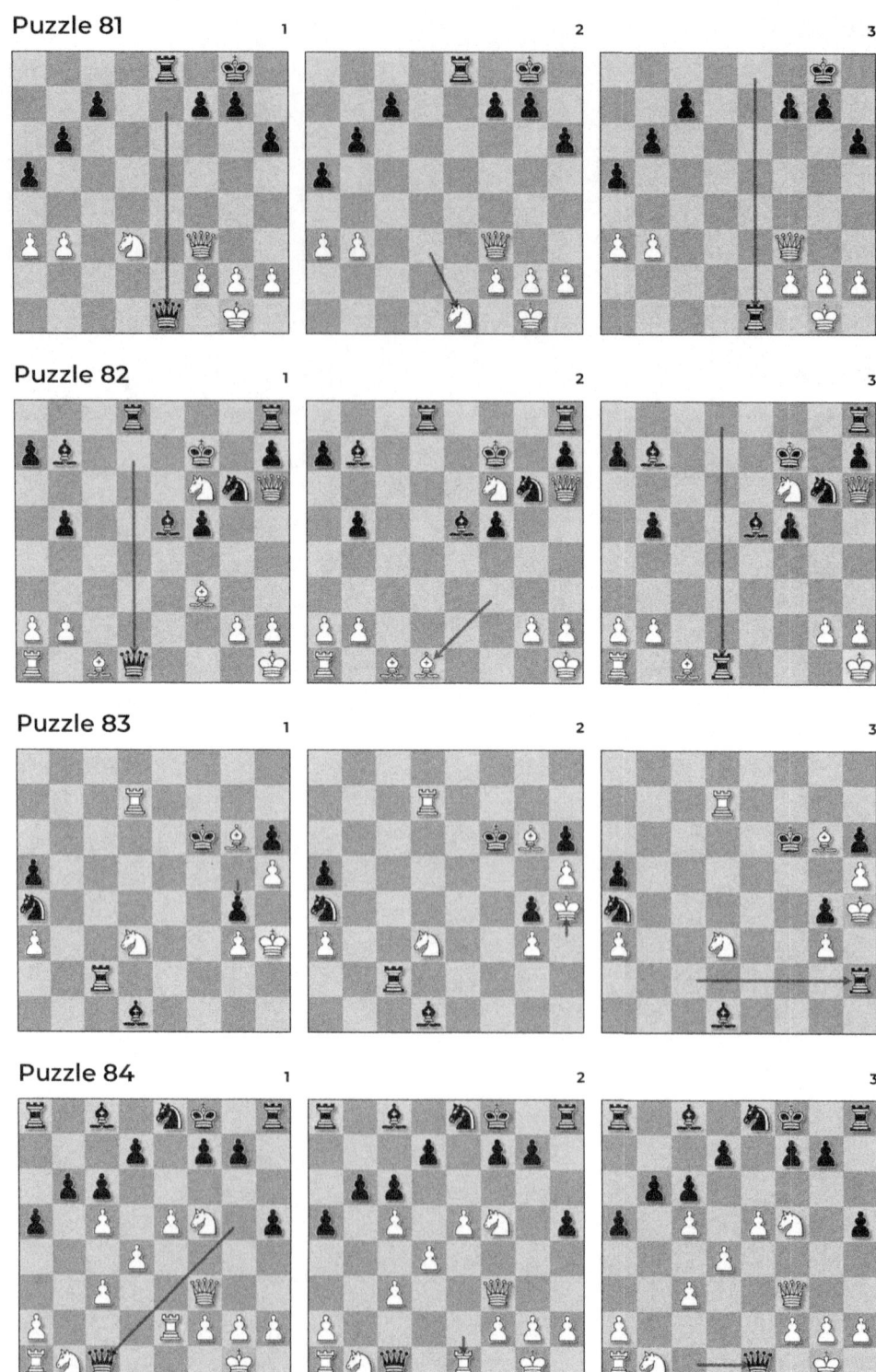

SOLUTIONS

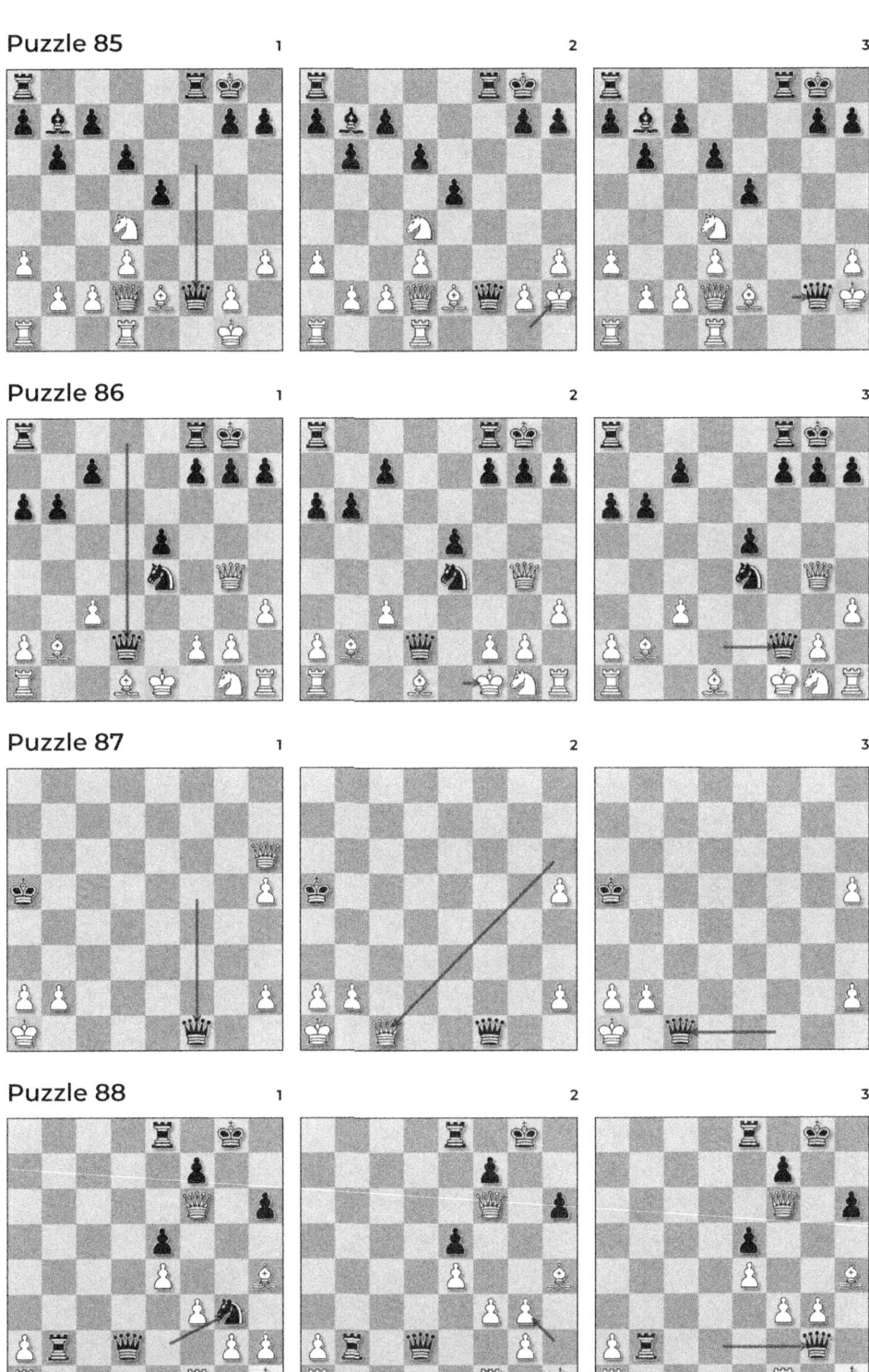

SOLUTIONS

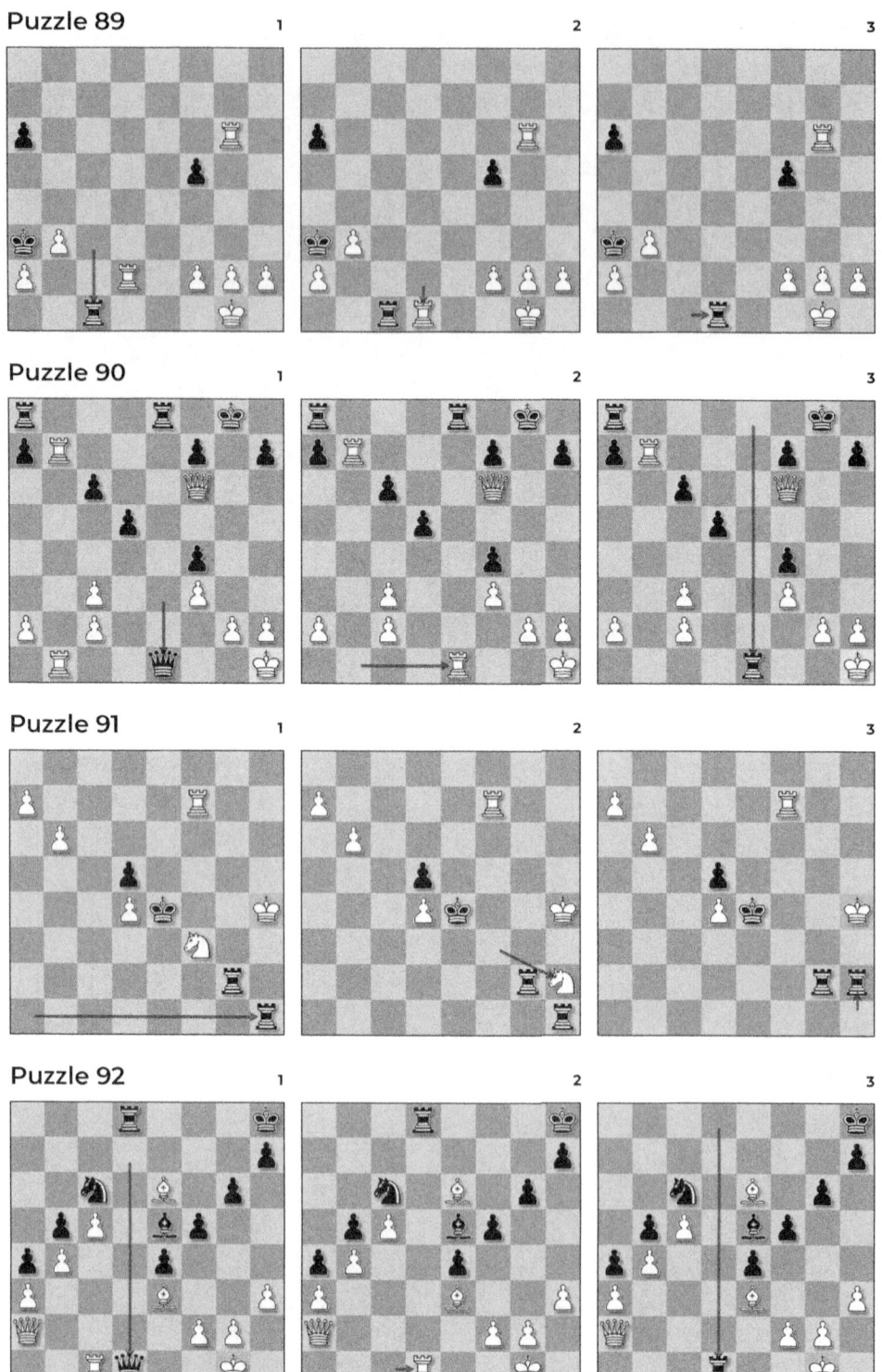

SOLUTIONS

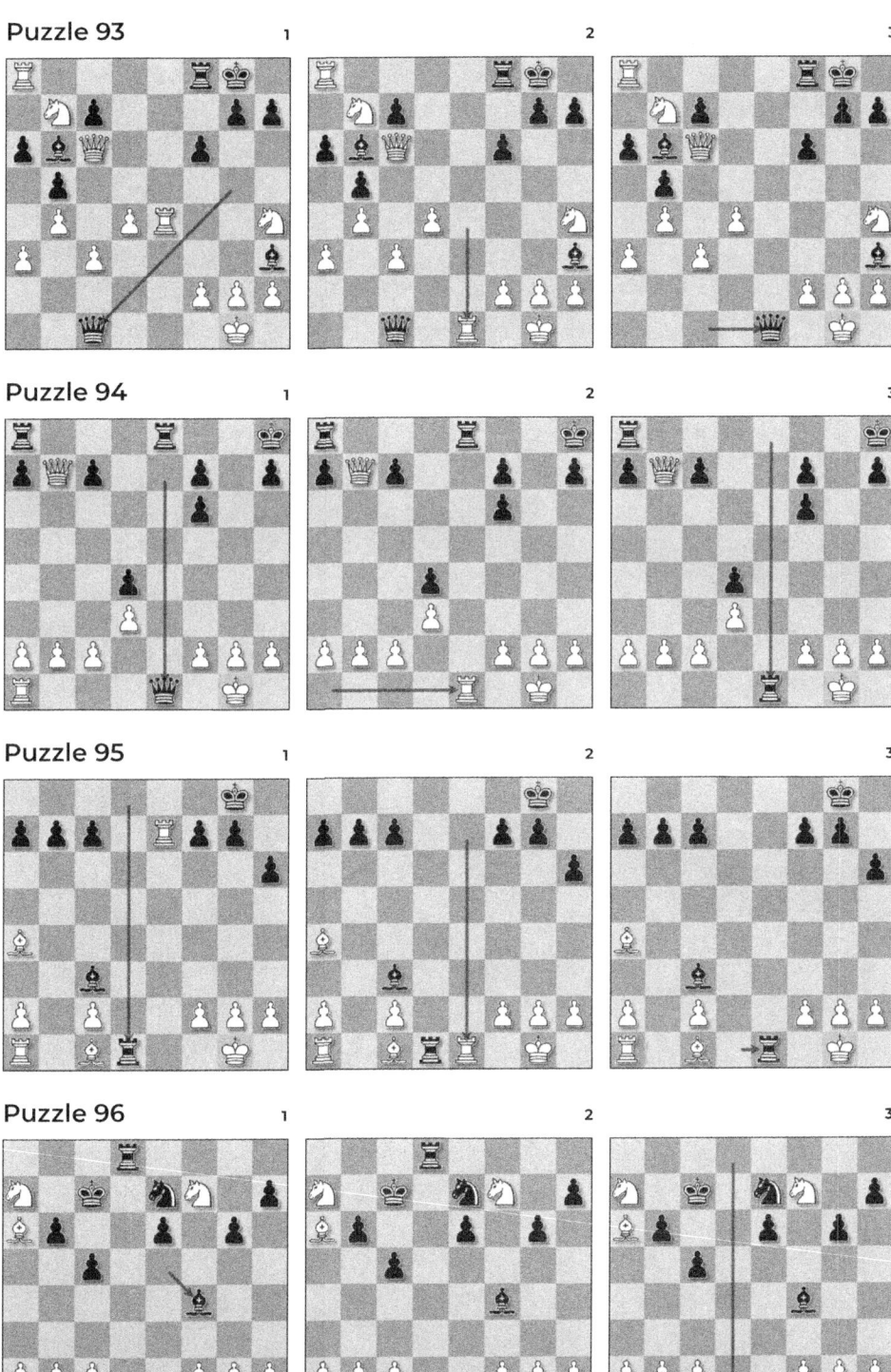

SOLUTIONS

Puzzle 97

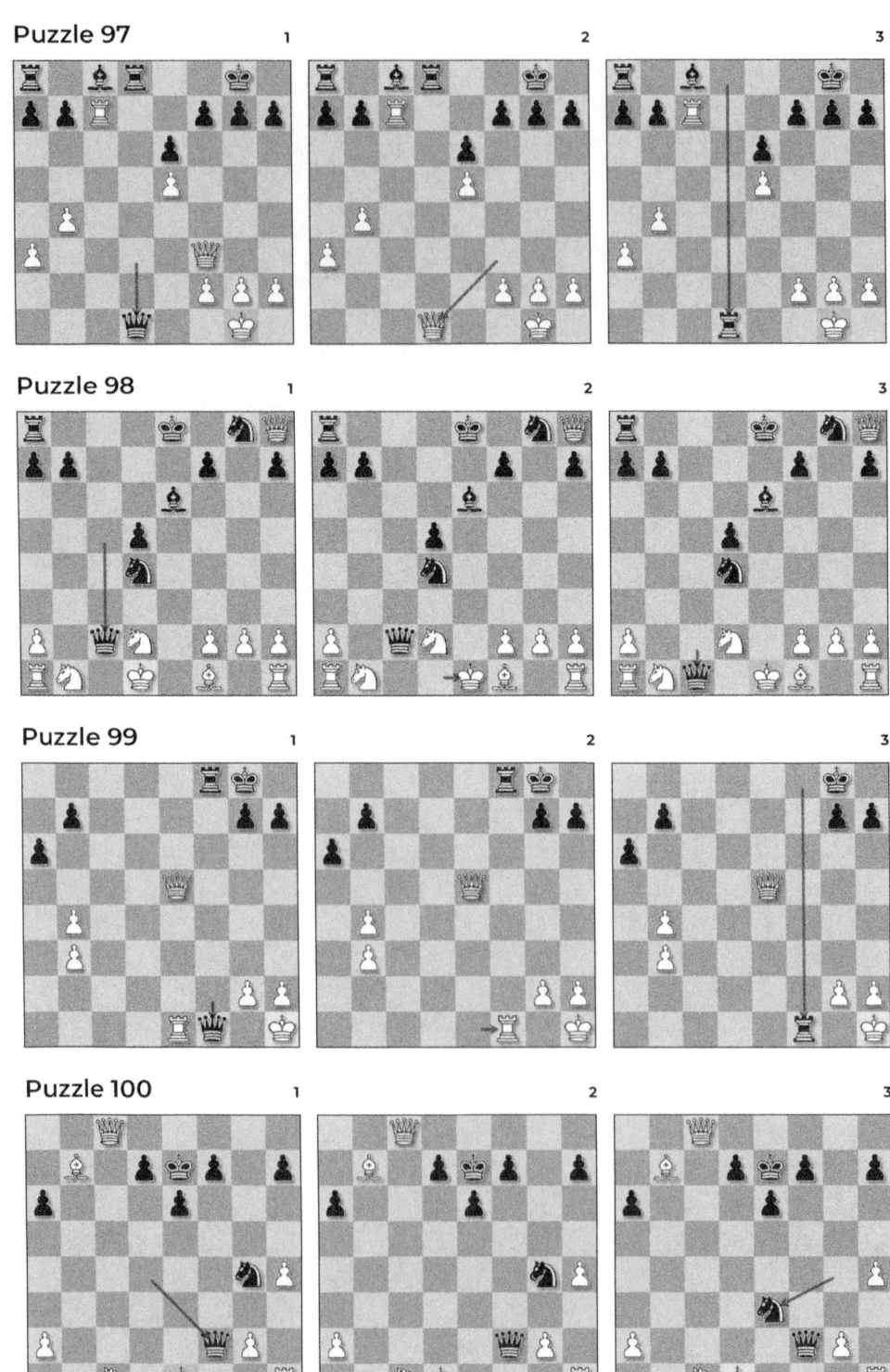

Puzzle 98

Puzzle 99

Puzzle 100

Printed in Great Britain
by Amazon